EASY PIANO

JAZZ STANDARDS
MADE EASY

ISBN 978-1-4803-0868-8

HAL•LEONARD®
CORPORATION

7777 W. BLUEMOUND RD. P.O. BOX 13819 MILWAUKEE, WI 53213

Visit Hal Leonard Online at
www.halleonard.com

CONTENTS

4 ALONE TOGETHER

7 AS TIME GOES BY

10 AT LAST

13 BEGIN THE BEGUINE

20 THE BEST IS YET TO COME

26 BLUE MOON

34 CHATTANOOGA CHOO CHOO

40 CUTE

31 DAYS OF WINE AND ROSES

42 EMILY

46 GENTLE RAIN

54 HOW ABOUT YOU?

58 IF YOU COULD SEE ME NOW

62 IN YOUR OWN SWEET WAY

49 IT HAD TO BE YOU

64 IT'S YOU OR NO ONE

70 JUMPIN' AT THE WOODSIDE

72 JUST FRIENDS

67 THE LAMP IS LOW

76 LAURA

86 LI'L DARLIN'

88 LOVE FOR SALE

92 MACK THE KNIFE

79 MINNIE THE MOOCHER

96 THE MORE I SEE YOU

102 THEME FROM "NEW YORK, NEW YORK"

108 NIGHT AND DAY

99 NUAGES

112 ON GREEN DOLPHIN STREET

116 ONE O'CLOCK JUMP

118 OVER THE RAINBOW

126 THE SHADOW OF YOUR SMILE

130 SING, SING, SING

136 SPRING IS HERE

140 STAR EYES

123 SWEET GEORGIA BROWN

144 TAKING A CHANCE ON LOVE

148 TEA FOR TWO

151 YOU AND THE NIGHT AND THE MUSIC

156 YOU STEPPED OUT OF A DREAM

ALONE TOGETHER

Lyrics by HOWARD DIETZ
Music by ARTHUR SCHWARTZ

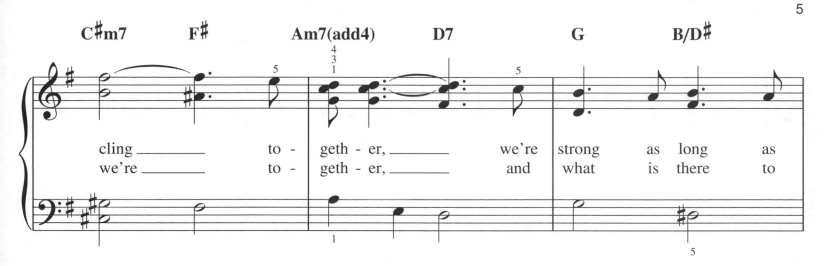

C#m7   F#   Am7(add4)   D7   G   B/D#

cling _____ to - | geth - er, _____ we're | strong as long as
we're _____ to - | geth - er, _____ and | what is there to

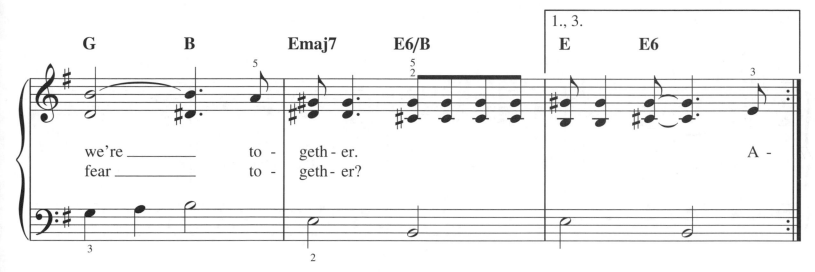

G   B   Emaj7   E6/B   **1., 3.** E   E6

we're _____ to - | geth - er.
fear _____ to - | geth - er?
A -

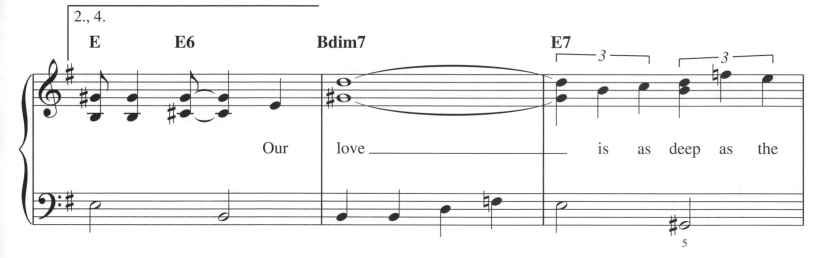

2., 4. E   E6   Bdim7   E7   3   3

Our | love _____ | is as deep as the

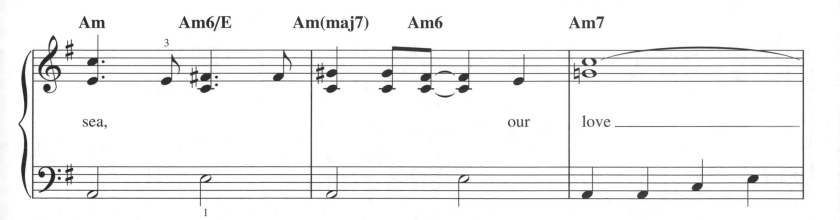

Am   Am6/E   Am(maj7)   Am6   Am7

sea, | our | love _____

is as great as a love _____ can be; _____ and

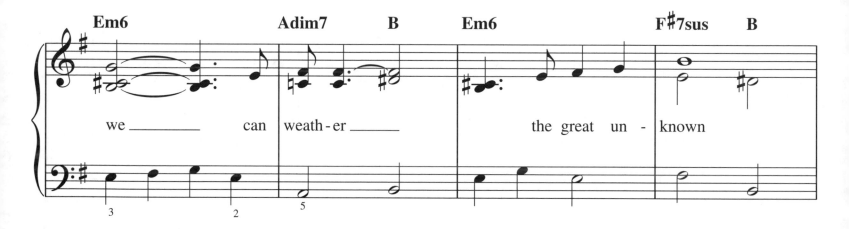

we _____ can weath-er _____ the great un - known

To Coda

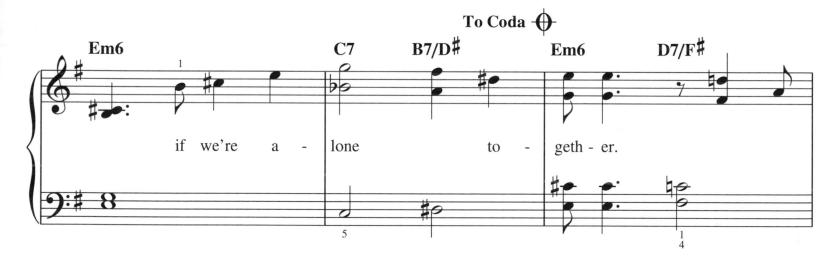

if we're a - lone to - geth-er.

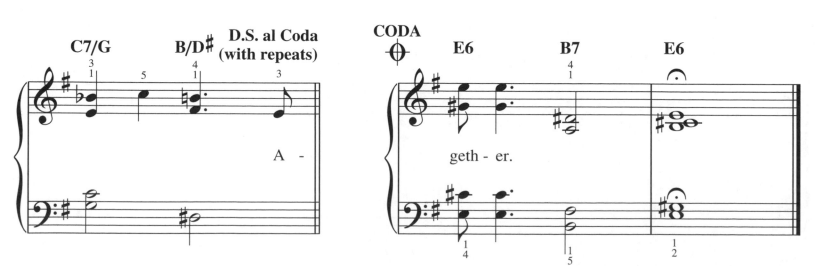

D.S. al Coda
(with repeats)

A -

CODA

geth - er.

AS TIME GOES BY

from CASABLANCA

Words and Music by
HERMAN HUPFELD

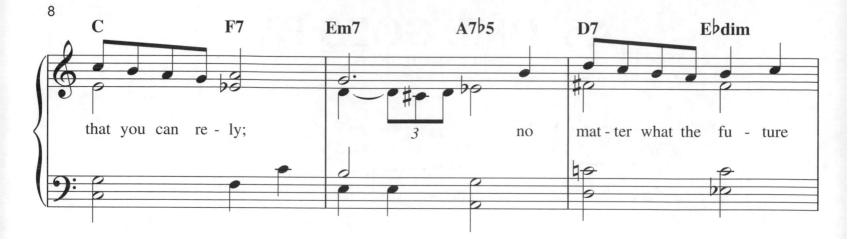

that you can re - ly; no mat - ter what the fu - ture

brings, as time goes by.

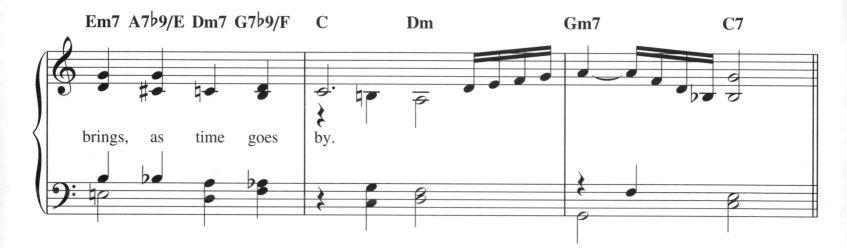

Moon-light and love _ songs nev - er out of date, hearts full of pas - sion,

jeal-ous-y and hate; wom-an needs man and man must have his mate, that

no one can de - ny. It's still the same old sto - ry, a

fight for love and glo - ry, a case of do or die! The

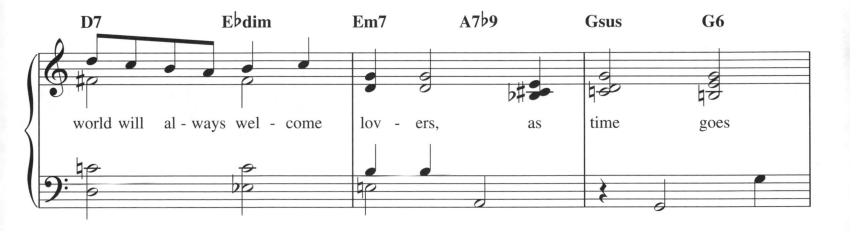

world will al - ways wel - come lov - ers, as time goes

1. by.

2. by.

AT LAST

Lyric by MACK GORDON
Music by HARRY WARREN

Slow Swing

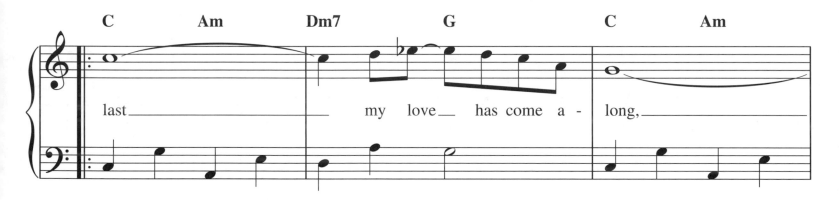

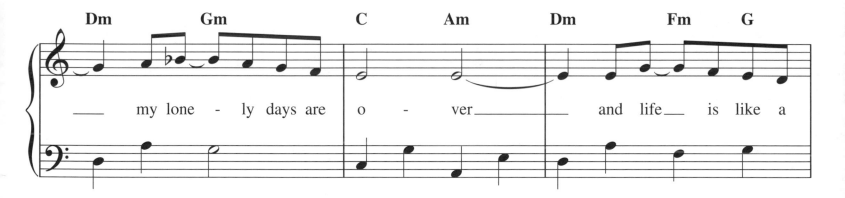

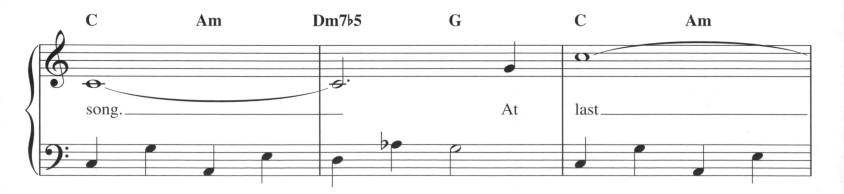

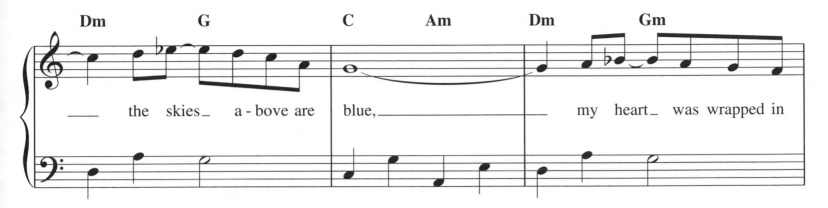

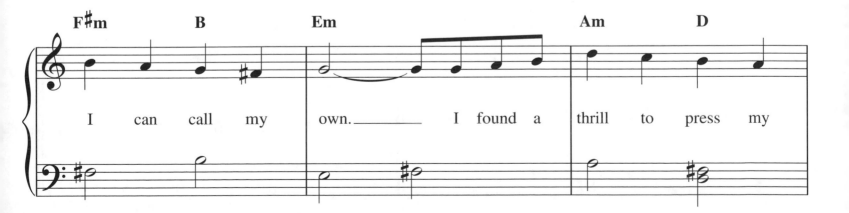

cheek to,   a   thrill I've nev - er   known.   You

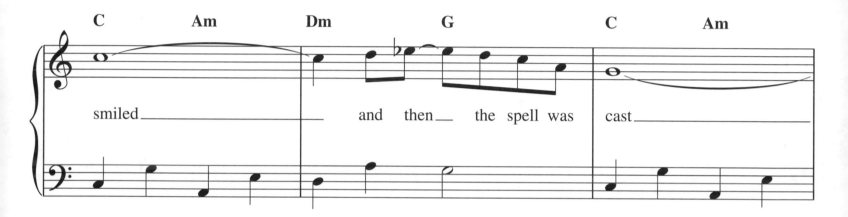

smiled_____ and then__ the spell was cast_____

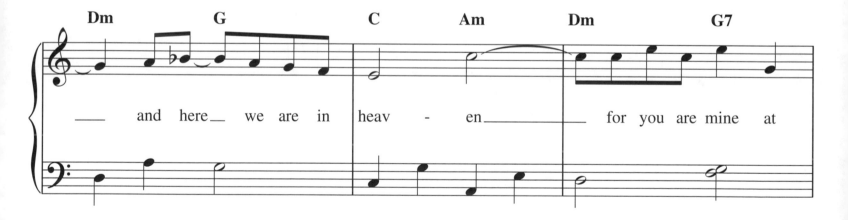

____ and here__ we are in heav - en_____ for you are mine at

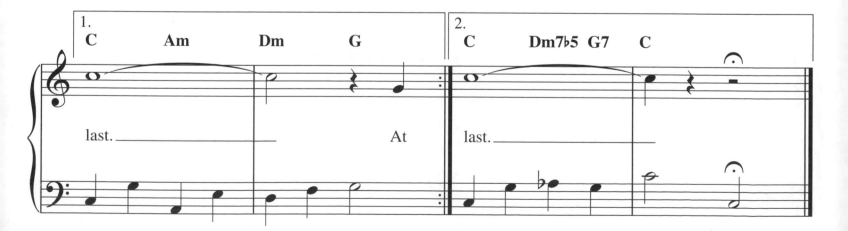

last._____   At   last._____

BEGIN THE BEGUINE
from JUBILEE

Words and Music by
COLE PORTER

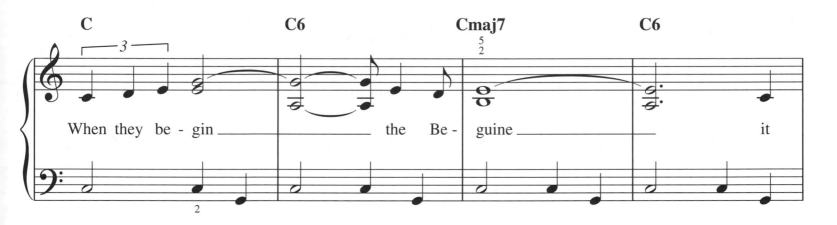

When they be - gin _____ the Be - guine _____ it

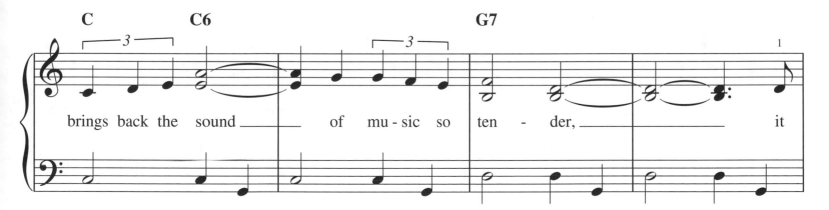

brings back the sound _____ of mu - sic so ten - der, _____ it

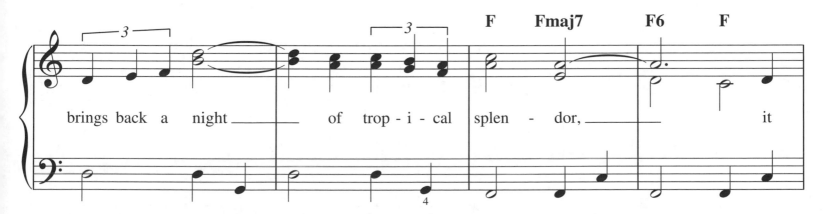

brings back a night _____ of trop - i - cal splen - dor, _____ it

brings back a mem - o - ry ev - er green. _____ I'm

with you once more _____ un - der the stars, _____ and

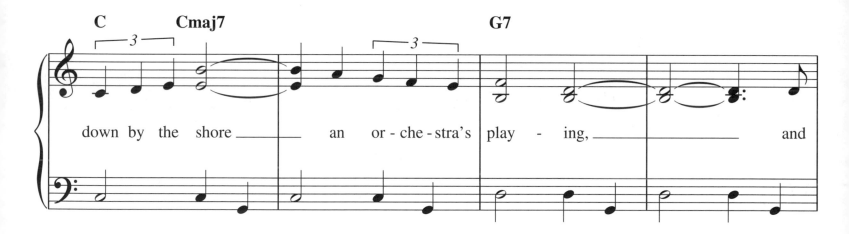

down by the shore _____ an or - che - stra's play - ing, _____ and

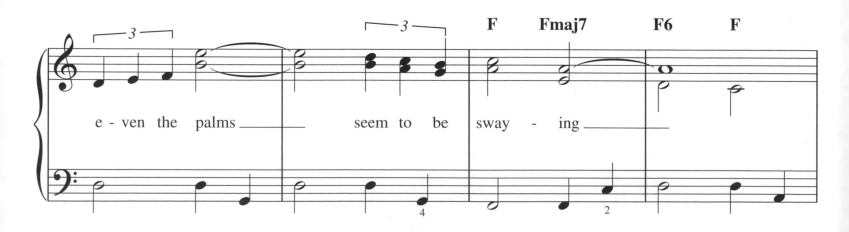

e - ven the palms _____ seem to be sway - ing _____

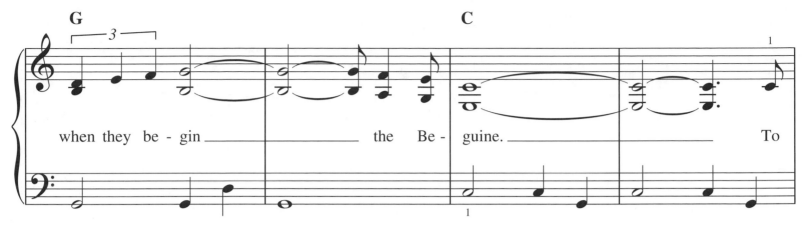

when they be - gin _____ the Be - guine. _____ To

live it a - gain _____ is past all en - deav - or, _____ ex -

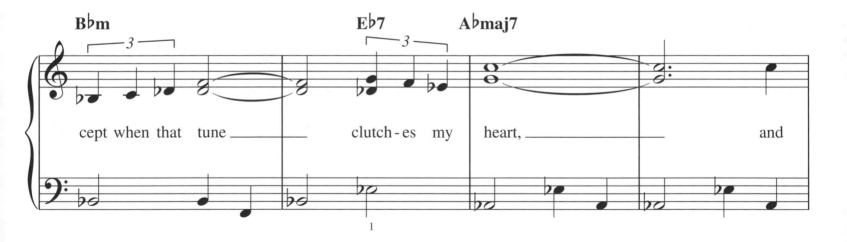

cept when that tune _____ clutch - es my heart, _____ and

there we are, swear - ing to love for - ev - er, and prom - is - ing

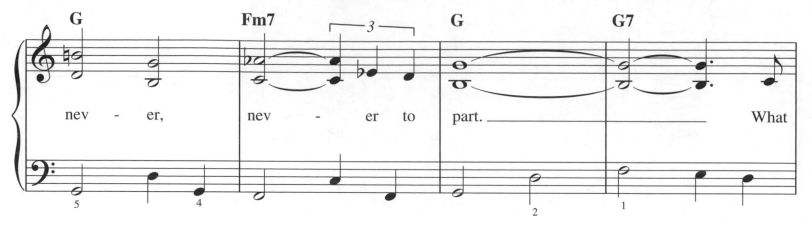

nev - er, nev - er to part. _____ What

mo - ments di - vine, _____ what rap - ture se - rene, _____ till

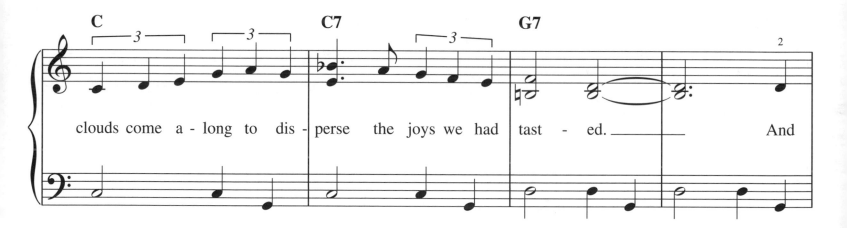

clouds come a - long to dis - perse the joys we had tast - ed. _____ And

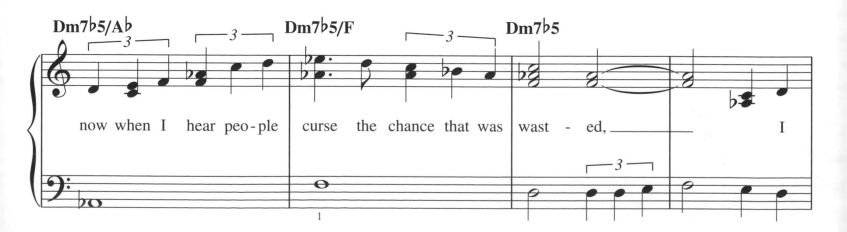

now when I hear peo - ple curse the chance that was wast - ed, _____ I

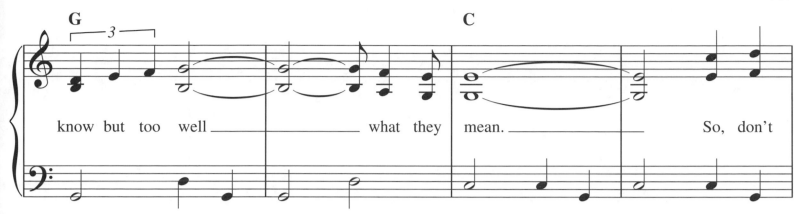

know but too well _____ what they mean. _____ So, don't

let them be - gin _____ the Be - guine. _____ Let the

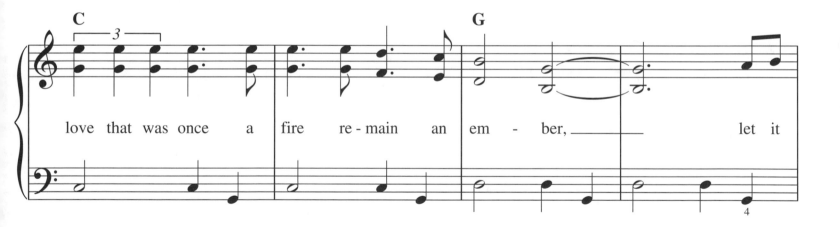

love that was once a fire re - main an em - ber, _____ let it

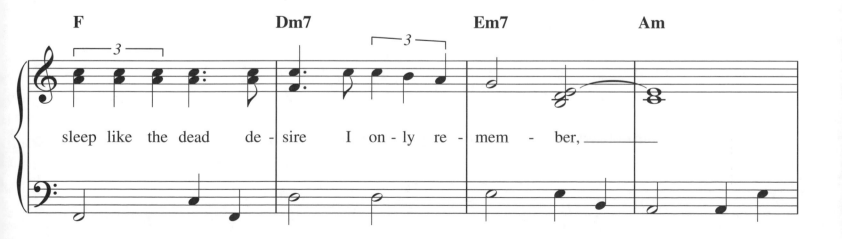

sleep like the dead de - sire I on - ly re - mem - ber, _____

when they be - gin _____ the Be - guine. _____ Oh yes,

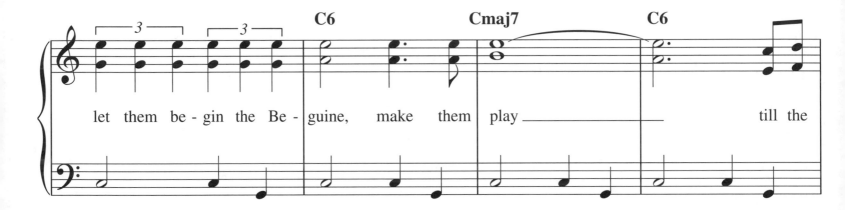

let them be - gin the Be - guine, make them play _____ till the

stars that were there be - fore re - turn a - bove you, _____ till you

whis - per to me once more, "Dar - ling, I love you," _____ and we

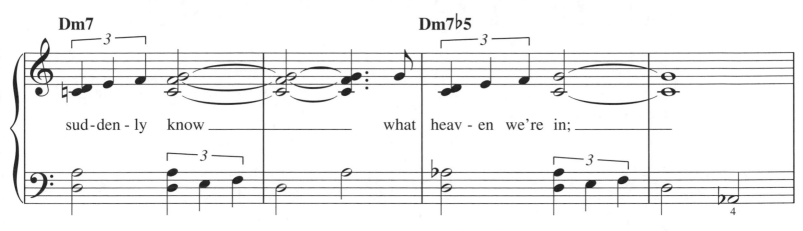

sud-den-ly know _____ what heav-en we're in; _____

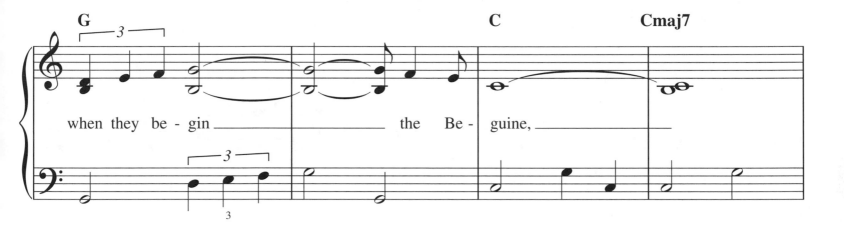

when they be-gin _____ the Be-guine, _____

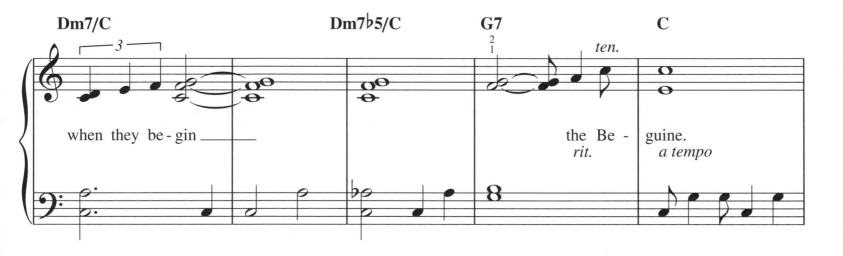

when they be-gin _____ the Be-guine.

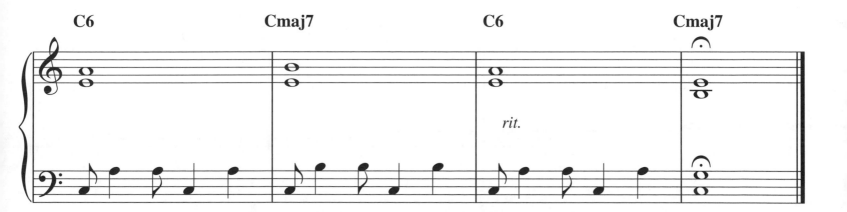

THE BEST IS YET TO COME

Music by CY COLEMAN
Lyrics by CAROLYN LEIGH

Big Band Swing

Out of the tree of life___ I just picked me a

plum.___

You came a-long and ev-

-'ry-thing's start-in' to hum.___

Wait till the warm-up's un-der-way, __ wait till our lips have met, __

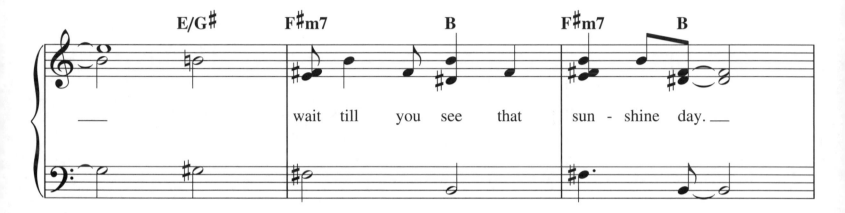

__ wait till you see that sun-shine day. __

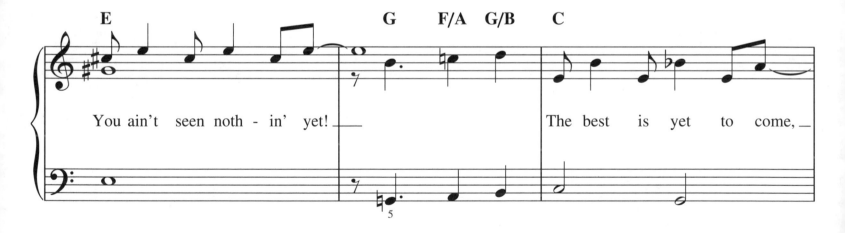

You ain't seen noth-in' yet! __ The best is yet to come, __

__ and, babe, won't it be fine? __

The best is yet to come, _ come the day _ you're mine.

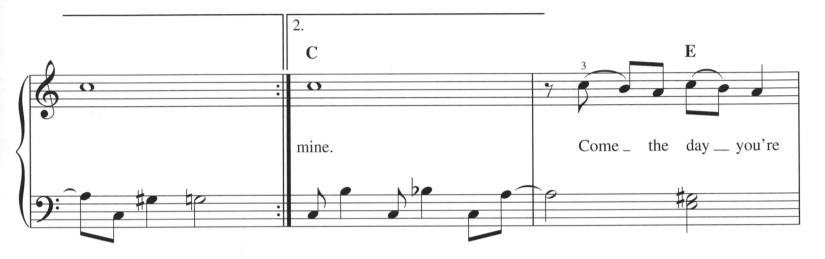

mine. Come _ the day _ you're

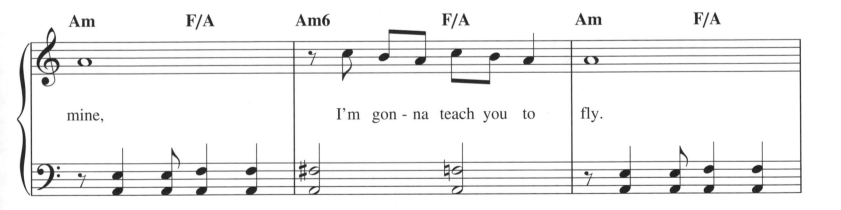

mine, I'm gon - na teach you to fly.

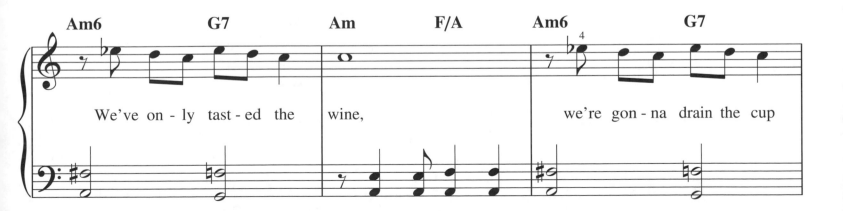

We've on - ly tast - ed the wine, we're gon - na drain the cup

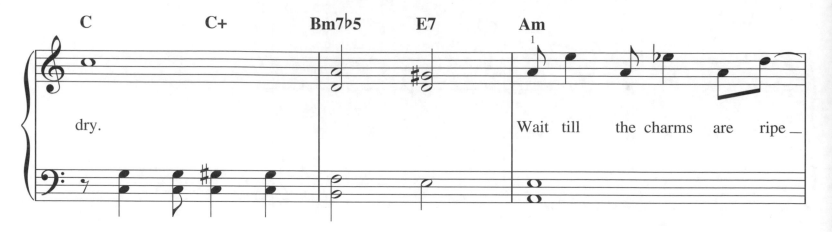

C C+ Bm7♭5 E7 Am

dry. Wait till the charms are ripe_

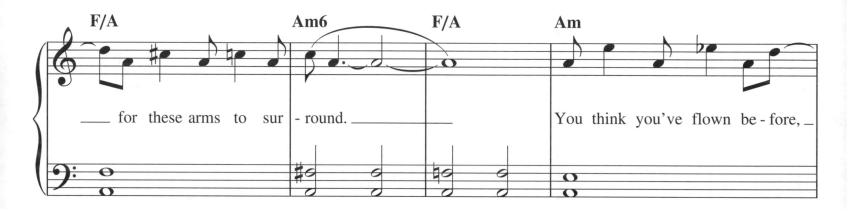

F/A Am6 F/A Am

_ for these arms to sur - round. _____ You think you've flown be - fore, _

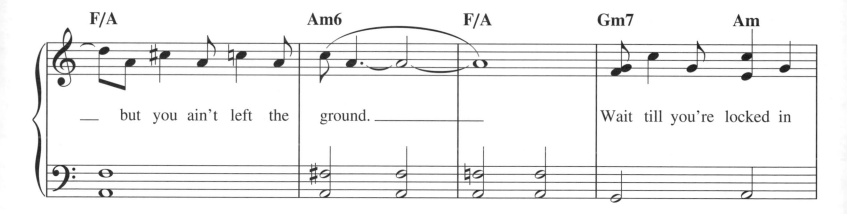

F/A Am6 F/A Gm7 Am

_ but you ain't left the ground. _____ Wait till you're locked in

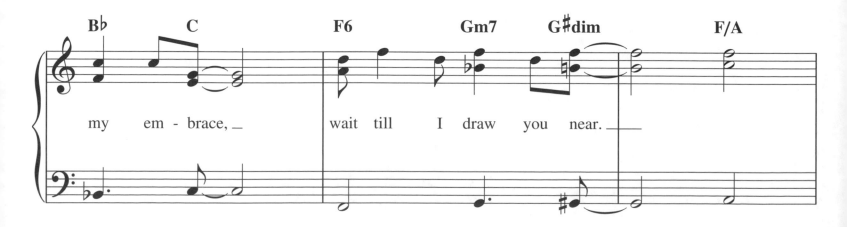

B♭ C F6 Gm7 G#dim F/A

my em - brace, _ wait till I draw you near._

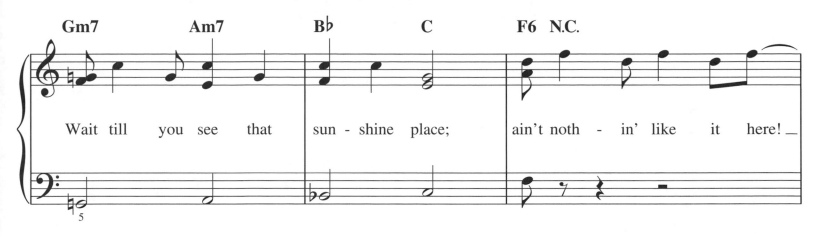

Gm7　Am7　B♭　C　F6　N.C.

Wait till you see that sun - shine place; ain't noth - in' like it here!

G　F/A　G/B　C

The best is yet to come ___ and, babe, won't it be

D7　G7

fine? _____ The best is yet to come, ___

C

___ come ___ the day ___ you're mine. _____

BLUE MOON

Music by RICHARD RODGERS
Lyrics by LORENZ HART

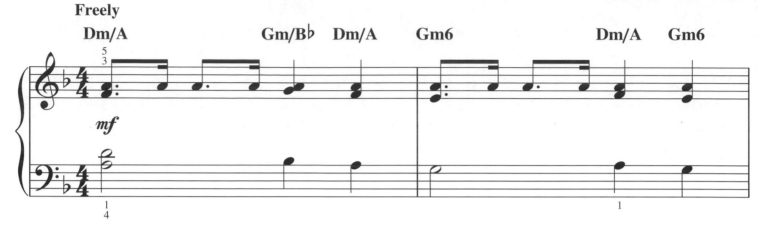

Once up-on a time, be - fore I took up smil - ing, I
Once up-on a time, my heart was just an or - gan; my

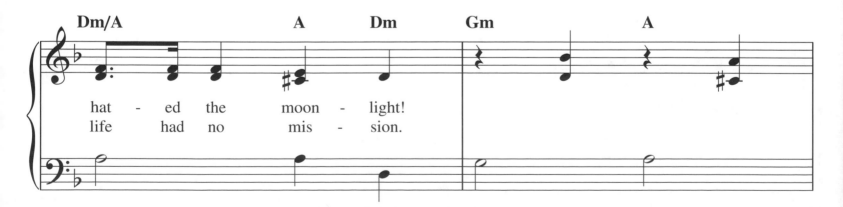

hat - ed the moon - light!
life had no mis - sion.

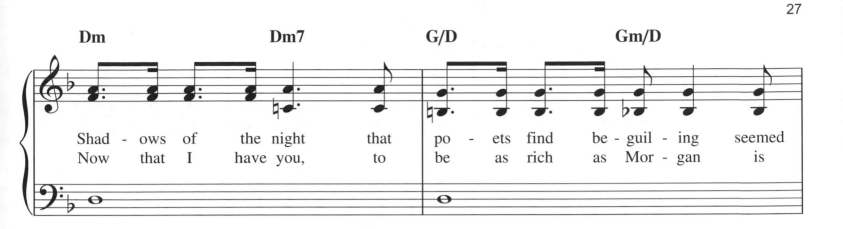

Shad - ows of the night that po - ets find be - guil - ing seemed
Now that I have you, that to be as rich as Mor - gan is

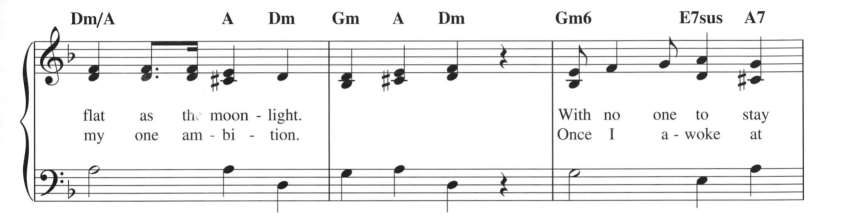

flat as the moon - light. With no one to stay
my one am - bi - tion. Once I a - woke at

up for, I went to sleep at ten.
sev - en, hat - ing the morn - ing light.

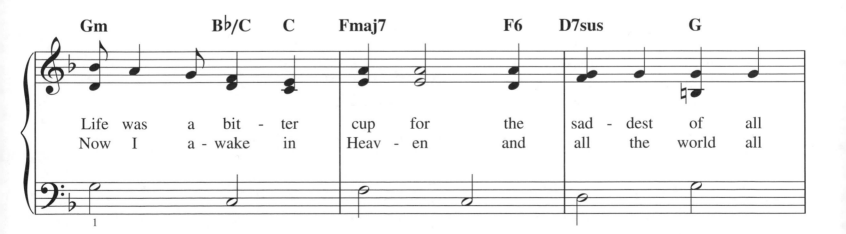

Life was a bit - ter cup for the sad - dest of all
Now I a - wake in Heav - en and all the world all

Relaxed Swing

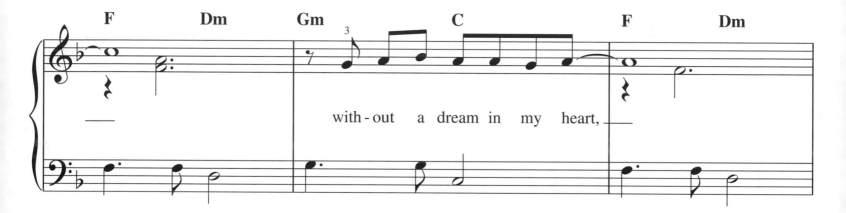

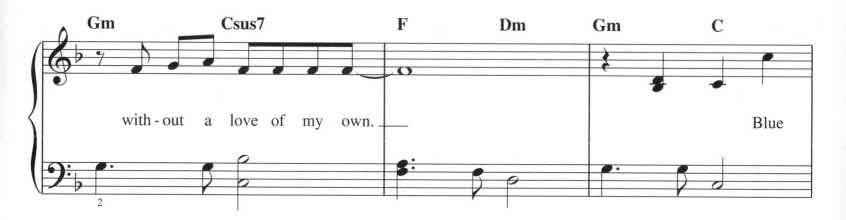

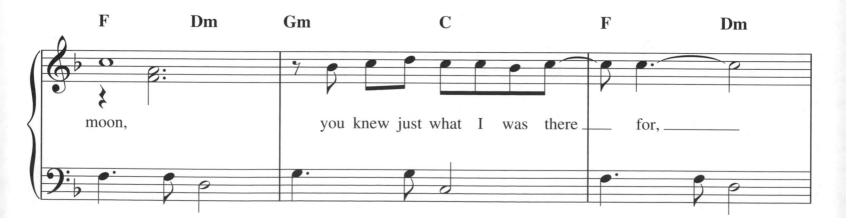

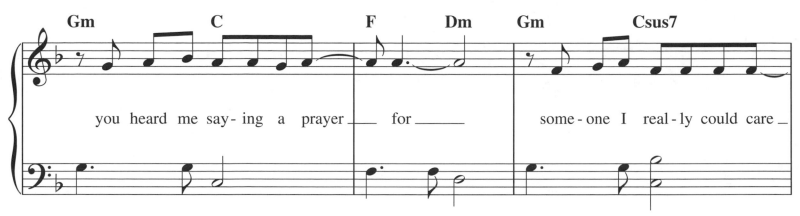

you heard me say-ing a prayer ___ for ___ some-one I real-ly could care ___

___ for. And then there sud-den-ly ap-peared be -

fore me ___ the on-ly one my arms will ev - er hold. ___ I heard some -

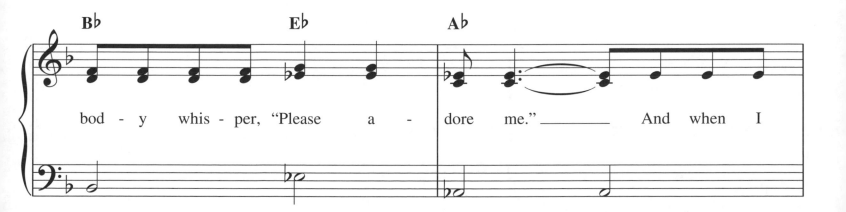

bod - y whis-per, "Please a - dore me." ___ And when I

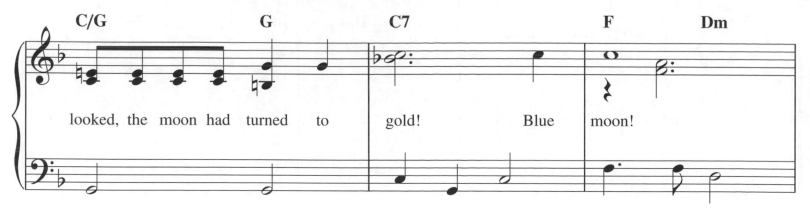

looked, the moon had turned to gold! Blue moon!

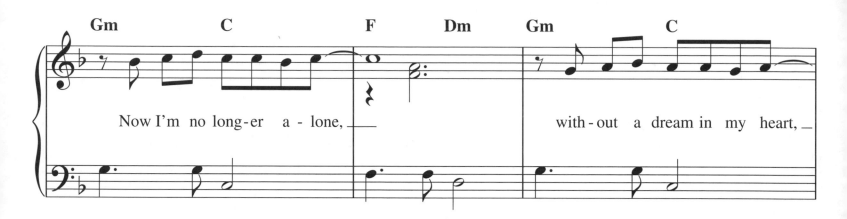

Now I'm no long-er a-lone, ___ with-out a dream in my heart, ___

with-out a love of my own. ___

rit. *rit.*

DAYS OF WINE AND ROSES

Lyrics by JOHNNY MERCER
Music by HENRY MANCINI

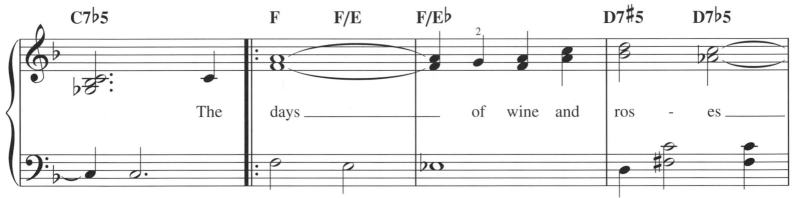

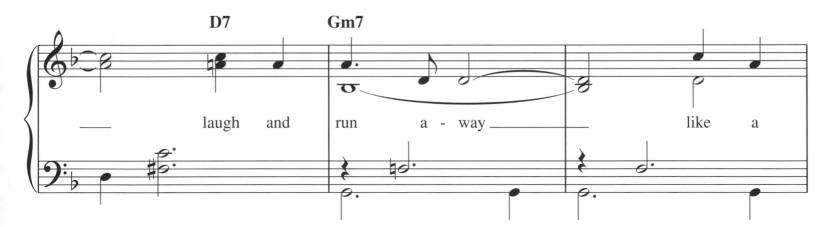

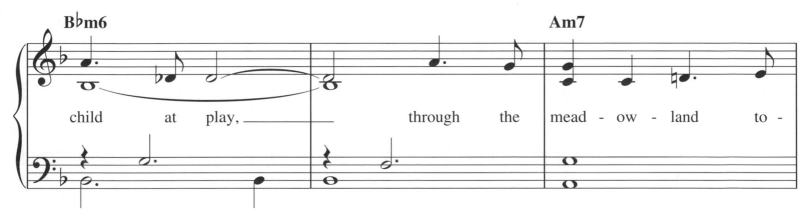

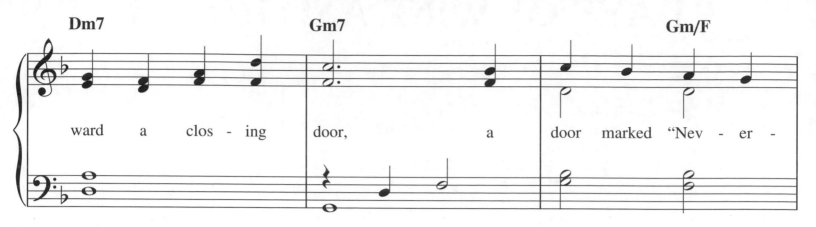

ward a clos - ing door, a door marked "Nev - er -

more," that was - n't there be - fore. The

lone - ly night dis - clos - es _____ just a

pass - ing breeze _____ filled with mem - o - ries _____

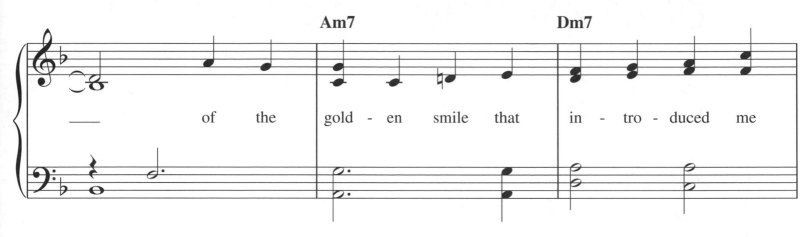

of the gold - en smile that in - tro - duced me

to _____ the days of wine and

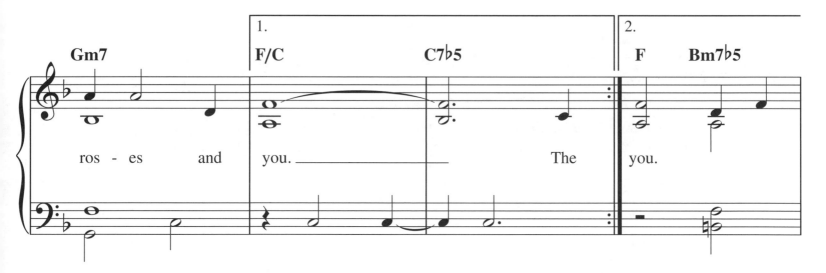

ros - es and you. _____ The you.

CHATTANOOGA CHOO CHOO

Words by MACK GORDON
Music by HARRY WARREN

Boogie, in 2

Par - don me, boy, _____
I can af - ford _____

is that the Chat - ta - noo - ga Choo Choo, _____
to board a Chat - ta - noo - ga Choo Choo. _____

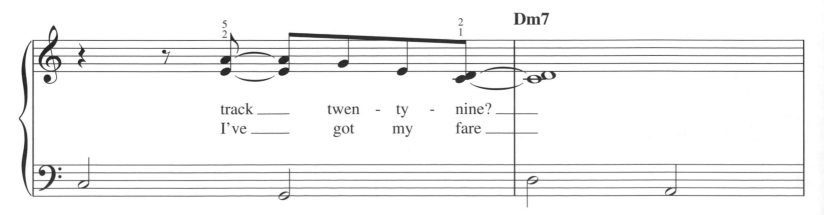

track _____ twen - ty nine? _____
I've _____ got my fare _____

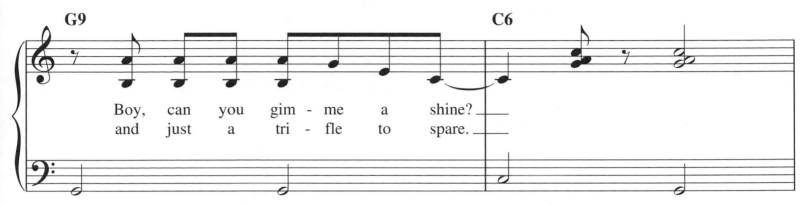

G9   **C6**

Boy, can you gim - me a shine?
and just a tri - fle to spare.

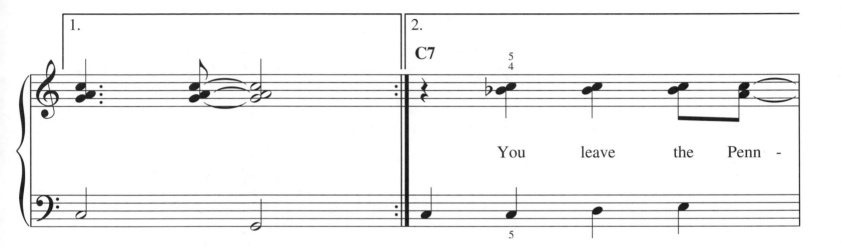

1.   **2.**   **C7**

You leave the Penn -

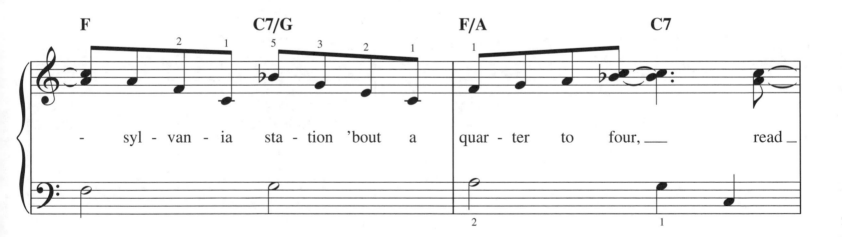

F   **C7/G**   **F/A**   **C7**

- syl - van - ia sta - tion 'bout a quar - ter to four, ___ read ___

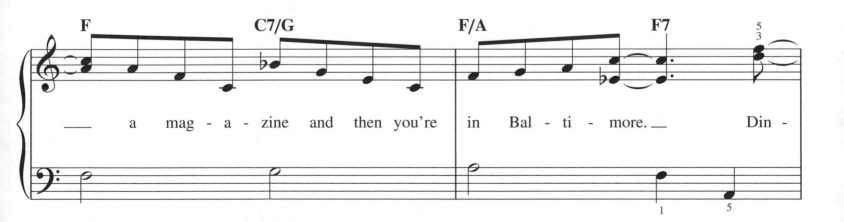

F   **C7/G**   **F/A**   **F7**

___ a mag - a - zine and then you're in Bal - ti - more. ___ Din -

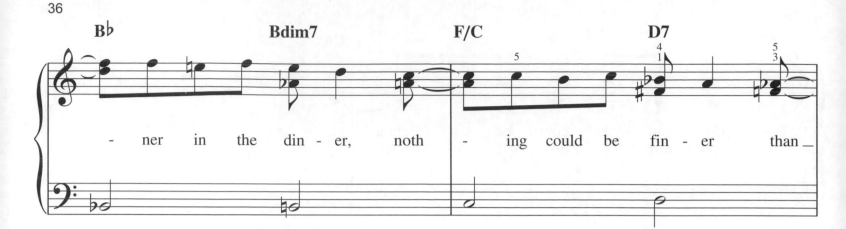

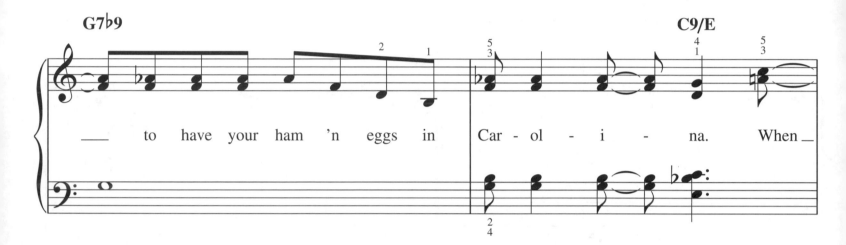

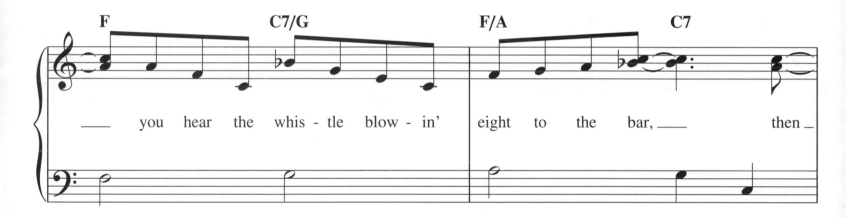

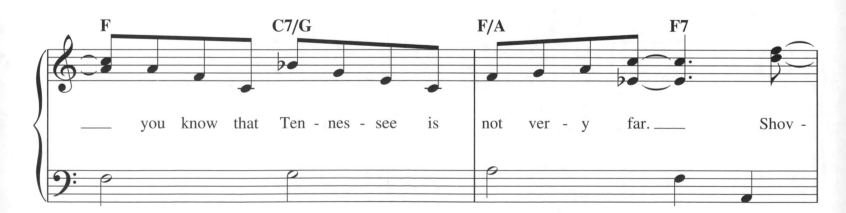

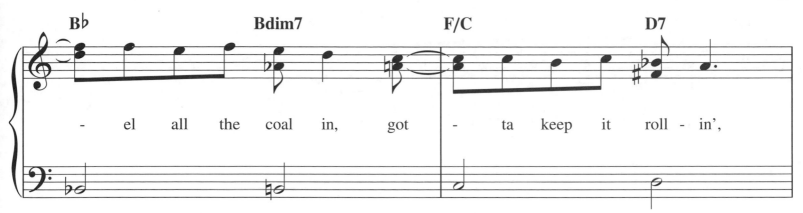

- el all the coal in, got - ta keep it roll - in',

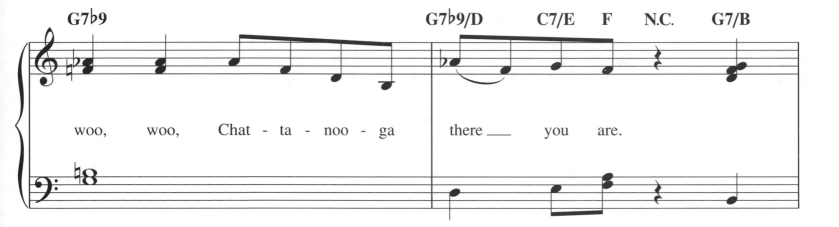

woo, woo, Chat - ta - noo - ga there ___ you are.

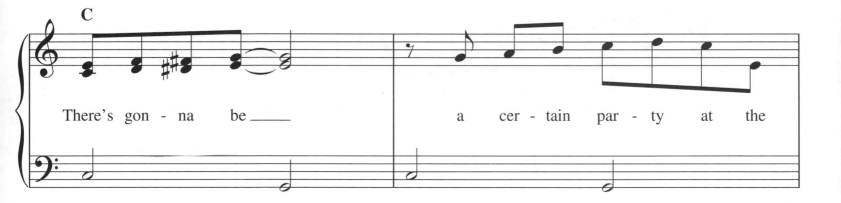

There's gon - na be ___ a cer - tain par - ty at the

sta - tion; ___ sat - in and lace, ___

G9   **C6**

I used to call "fun - ny face."

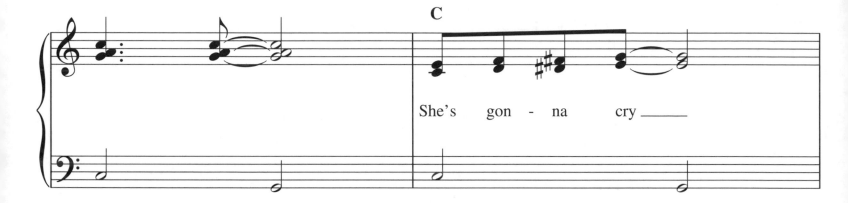

C

She's gon - na cry _____

C7/B♭   **F/A**

un - til I tell her that I'll nev - er roam. _____

A♭7   **C/G**   **Am7**

So Chat - ta - noo - ga Choo Choo,

won't you choo __ choo me home? __

Chat - ta - noo - ga Choo Choo, won't you choo __ choo me home?

CUTE

Music by NEAL HEFTI
Words by STANLEY STYNE

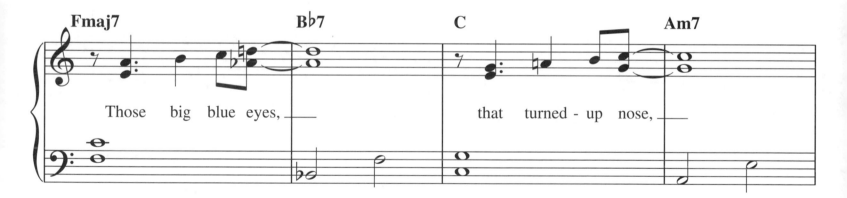

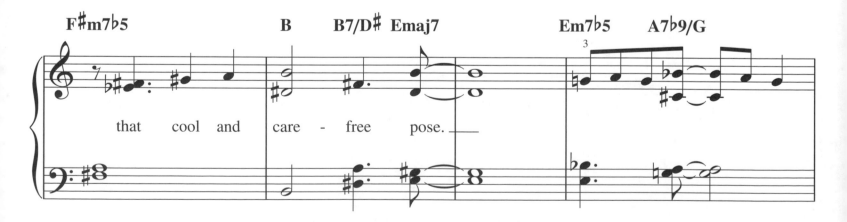

I mean, I   like   your   style,

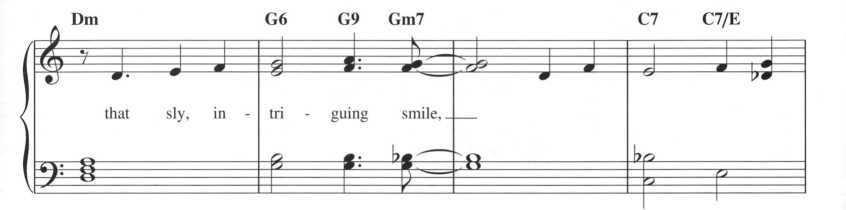

that   sly,   in - tri - guing   smile,____

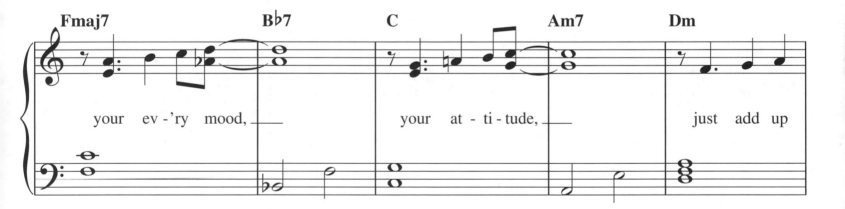

your   ev -'ry   mood,____   your   at - ti - tude,____   just   add   up

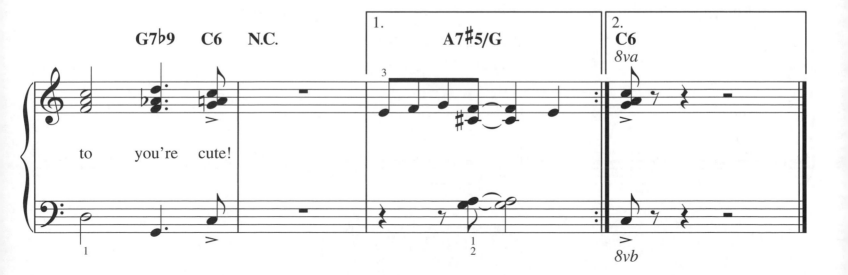

to   you're   cute!

EMILY

from the MGM Motion Picture THE AMERICANIZATION OF EMILY

Music by JOHNNY MANDEL
Words by JOHNNY MERCER

Moderately slow, with freedom

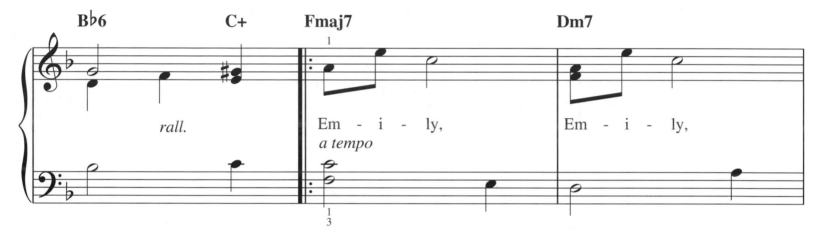

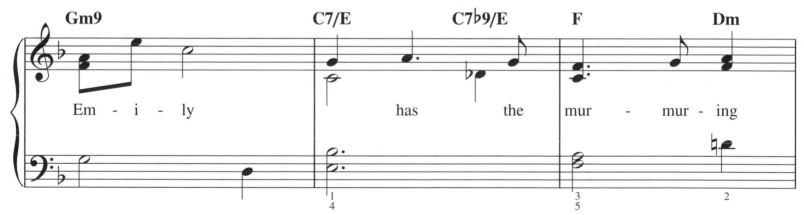

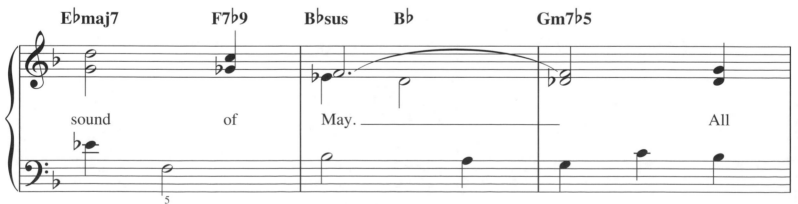

silver bells, coral shells, carousels,

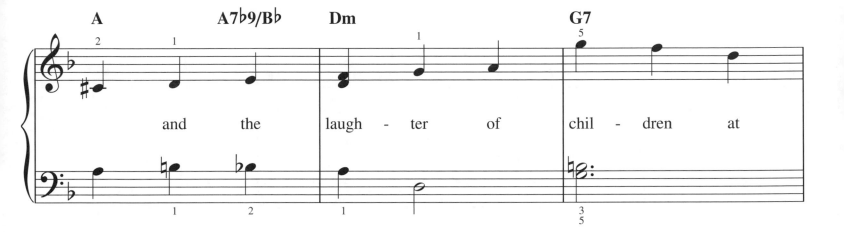

and the laughter of children at

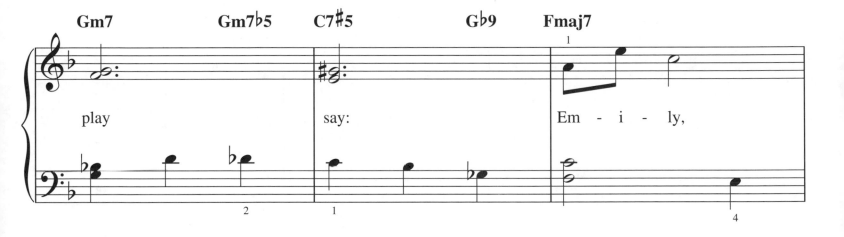

play say: Emily,

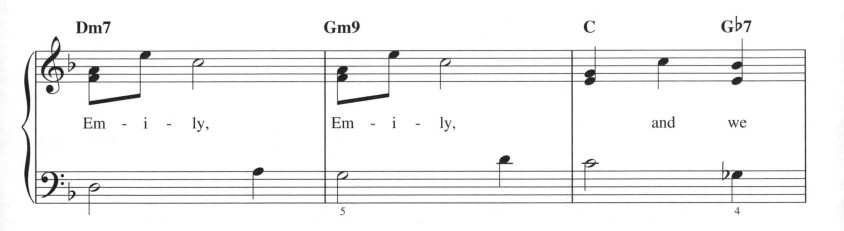

Emily, Emily, and we

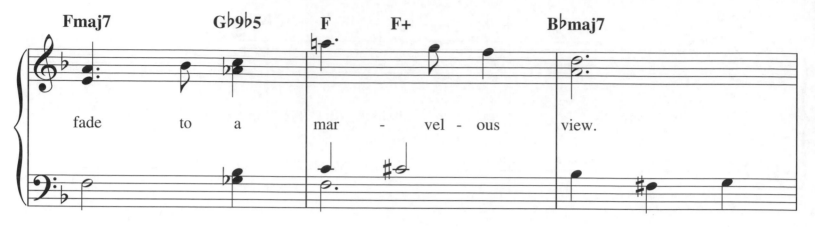

fade   to   a   mar -   vel - ous   view.

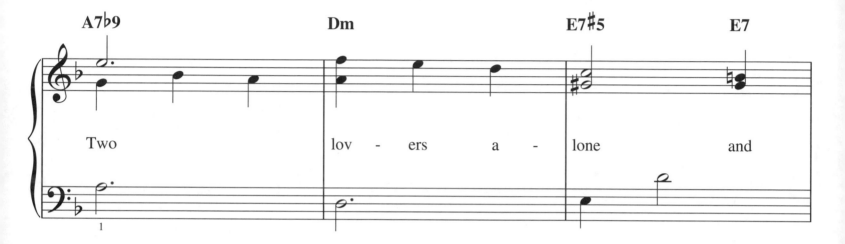

Two   lov - ers   a -   lone   and

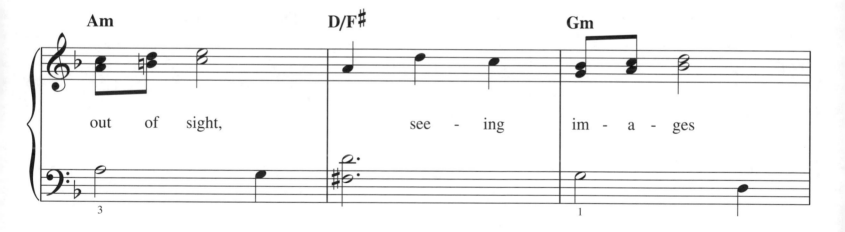

out   of   sight,   see - ing   im - a - ges

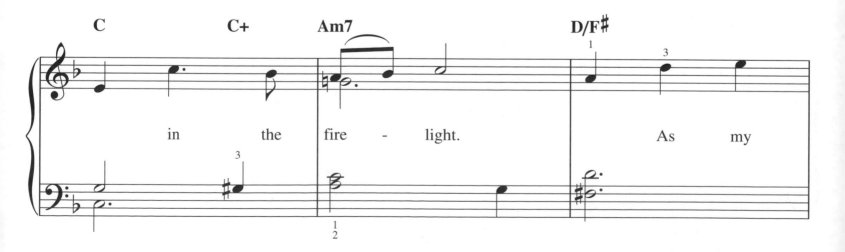

in   the   fire - light.   As   my

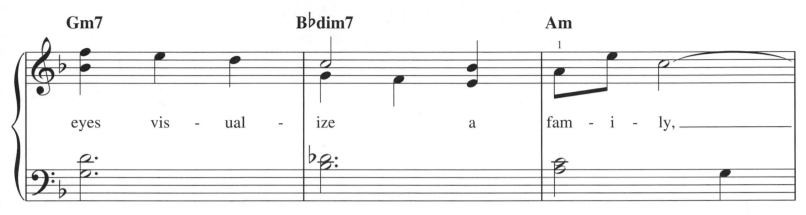

eyes   vis - ual - ize   a   fam - i - ly, _____

_____   they   see   dream - i - ly,   Em - i - ly,

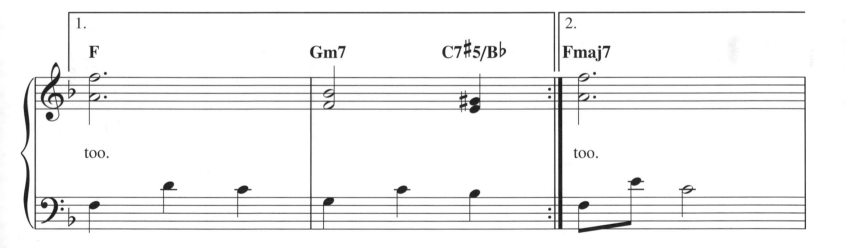

too.   too.

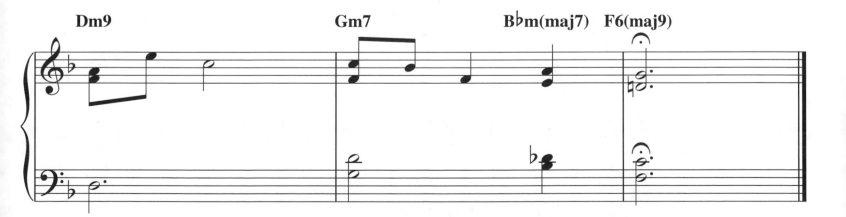

GENTLE RAIN
from the Motion Picture THE GENTLE RAIN

Music by LUIZ BONFA
Words by MATT DUBEY

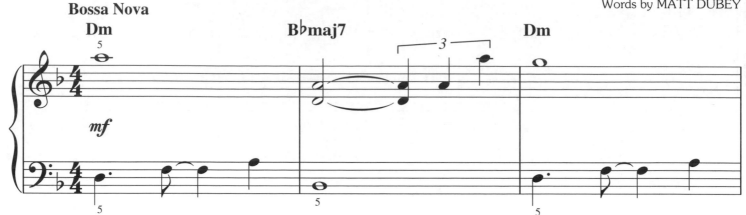

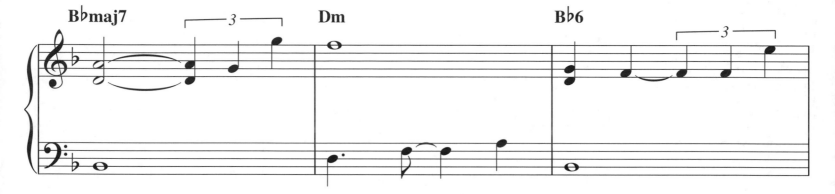

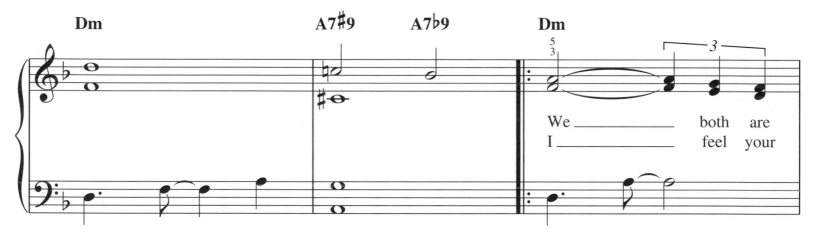

We _____ both are
I _____ feel your

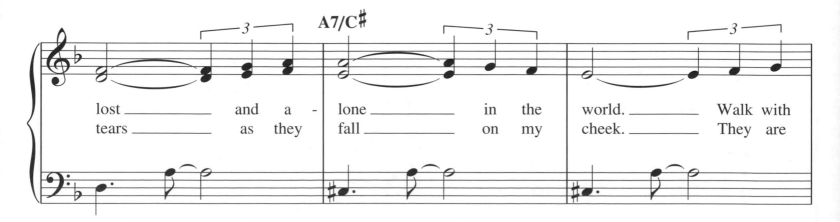

lost _____ and a-lone _____ in the world. _____ Walk with
tears _____ as they fall _____ on my cheek. _____ They are

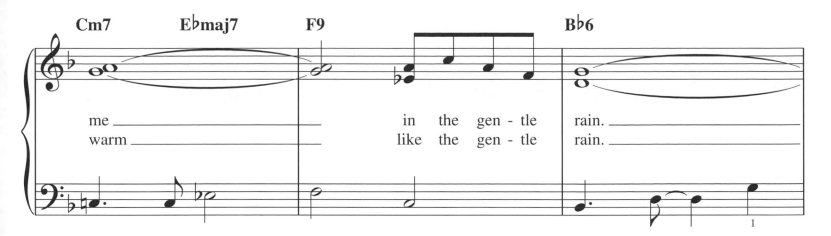

Cm7　　Ebmaj7　　F9　　Bb6

me _____ in the gen - tle rain. _____
warm _____ like the gen - tle rain. _____

Bm7b5　　E7

___ Don't _____ be a - fraid; _____ I've a
___ Come, _____ lit - tle one, _____ you've got

Am7b5　　D7　　Gm7b5

hand _____ for your hand, _____ and I will _____ be your
me _____ in the world, _____ and our love _____ will be

Em7b5　　A7　　Dm7　　A7b9

1.

love for a while.
sweet, ver - y

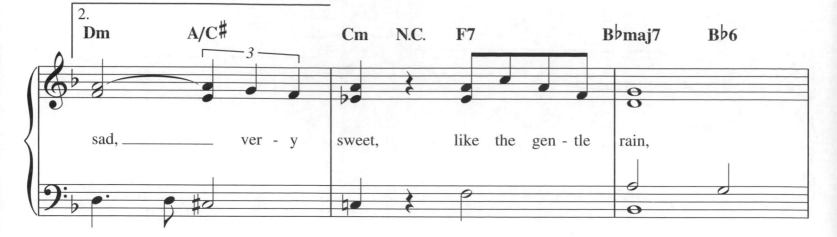

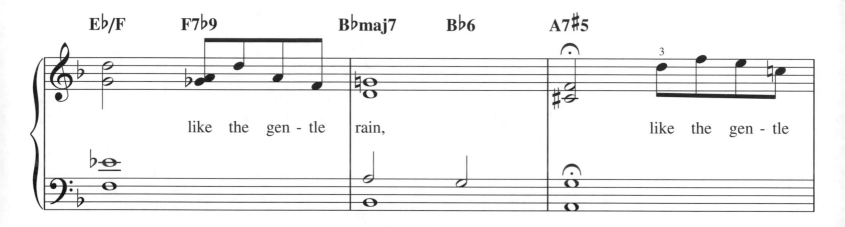

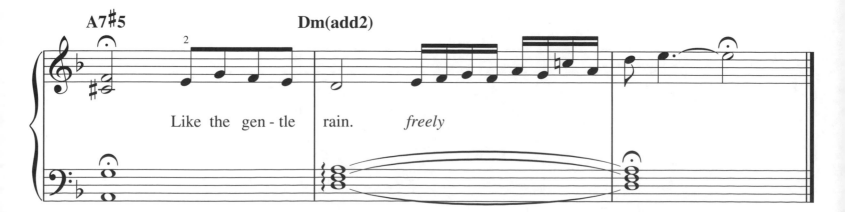

IT HAD TO BE YOU

Words by GUS KAHN
Music by ISHAM JONES

Moderate Swing

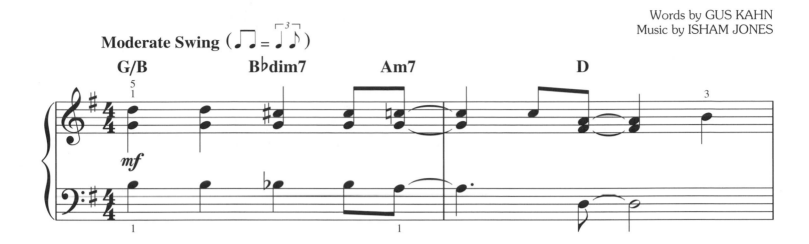

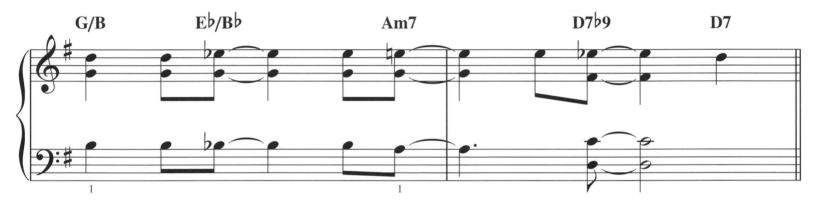

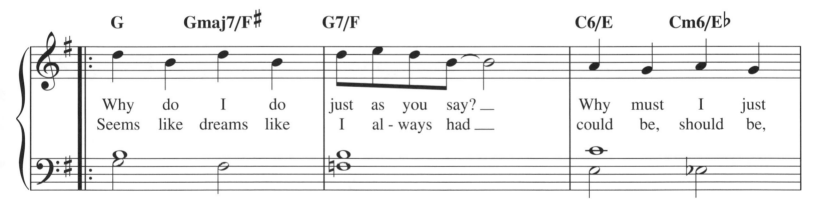

Why do I do just as you say? __ Why must I just could be, should be,
Seems like dreams like I al-ways had __

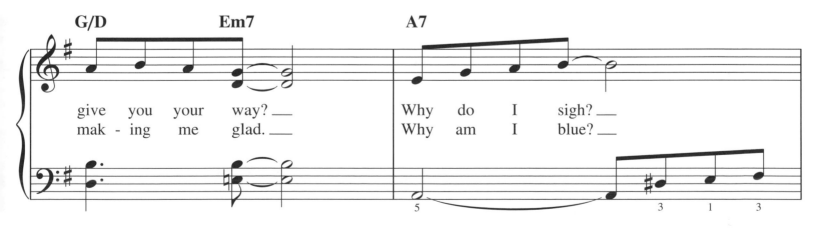

give you your way? __ Why do I sigh? __
mak-ing me glad. __ Why am I blue? __

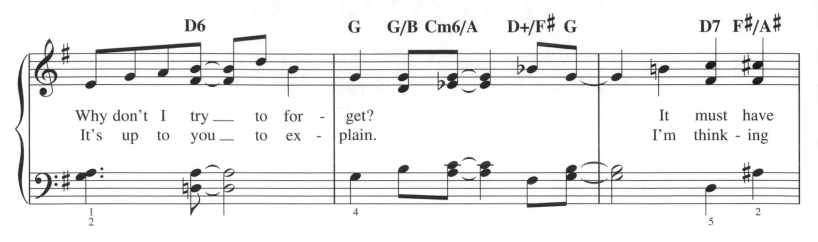

Why don't I try __ to for - get?
It's up to you __ to ex - plain.
It must have
I'm think - ing

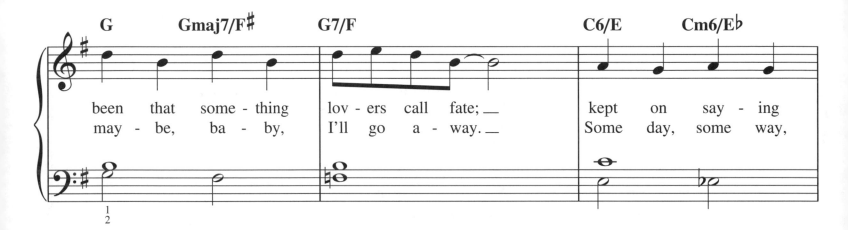

been that some - thing
may - be, ba - by,
lov - ers call fate; __
I'll go a - way. __
kept on say - ing
Some day, some way,

I had to wait. __
you'll come and say, __
I saw it all, __
"It's you I need," __
just could - n't fall __ till we
and you'll be plead - ing in

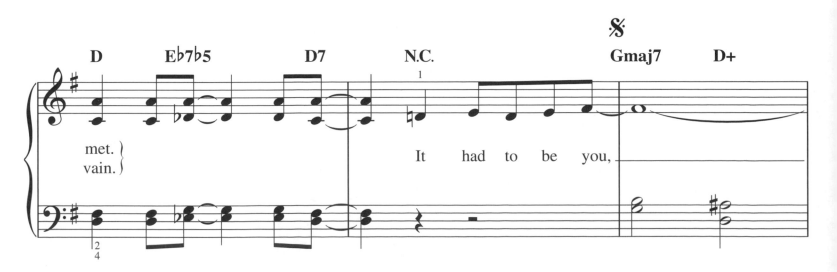

met.
vain.
It had to be you, _____

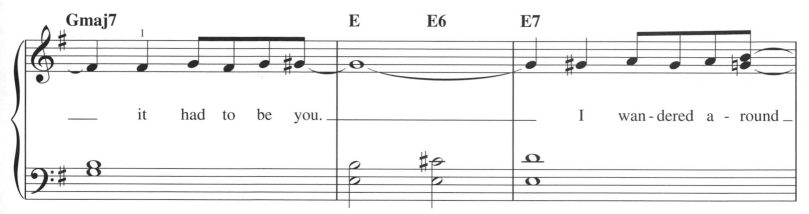

it had to be you. _____ I wan-dered a - round ___

___ and fi - nal - ly found ___ the some-bod - y who ___

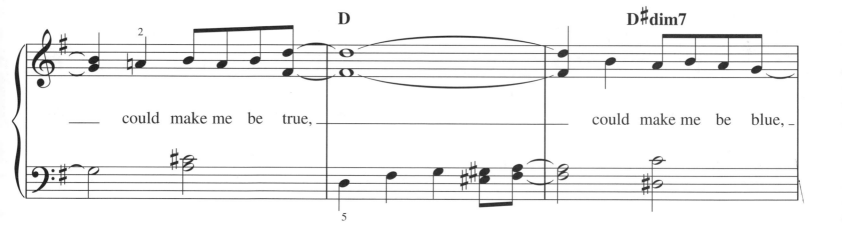

___ could make me be true, _____ could make me be blue, _

and e - ven be glad, ___ just to be sad, _

think-ing of you. Some oth-ers I've seen

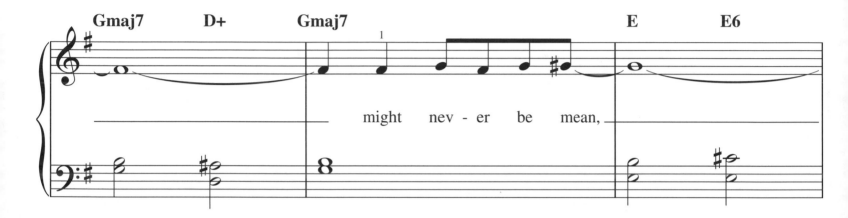

might nev-er be mean,

might nev-er be cross or try to be boss, but they would-n't do.

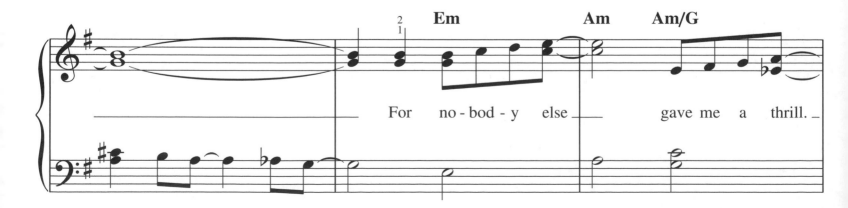

For no-bod-y else gave me a thrill.

With all your faults, ___ I love you still. ___ It had to be you, ___

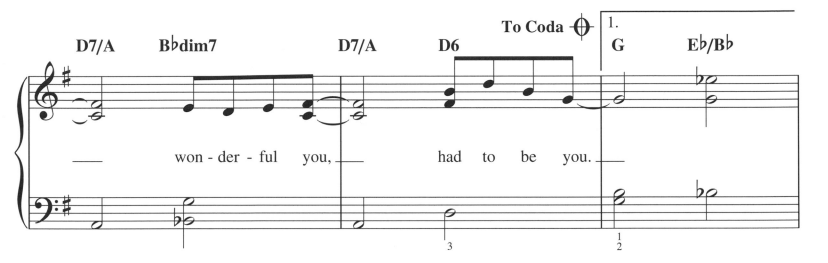

___ won - der - ful you, ___ had to be you. ___

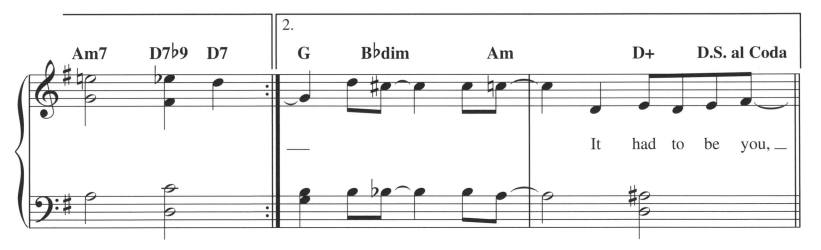

___ It had to be you, ___

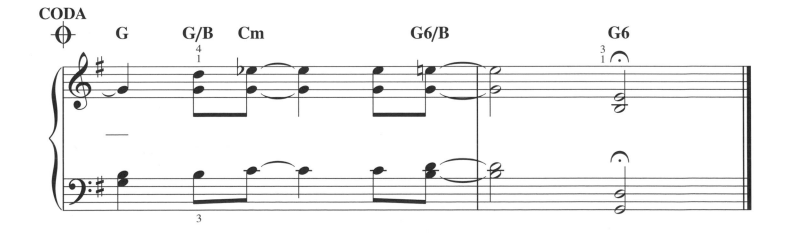

HOW ABOUT YOU?

Words by RALPH FREED
Music by BURTON LANE

Moderately, with freedom

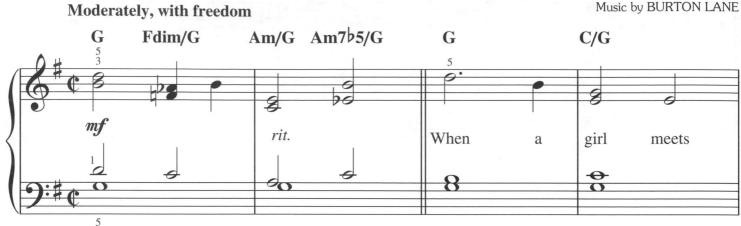

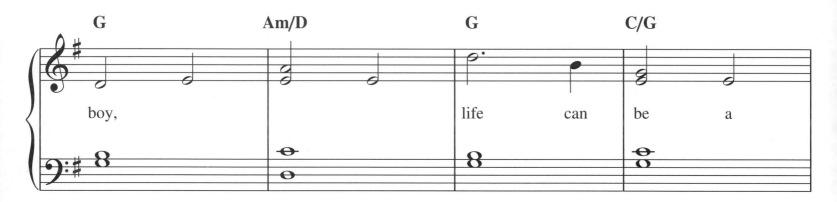

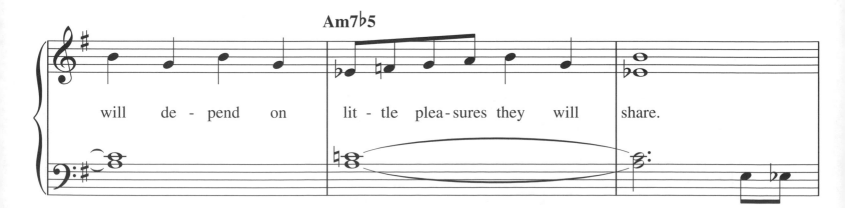

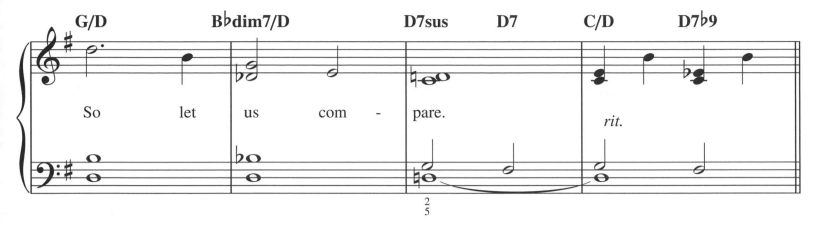

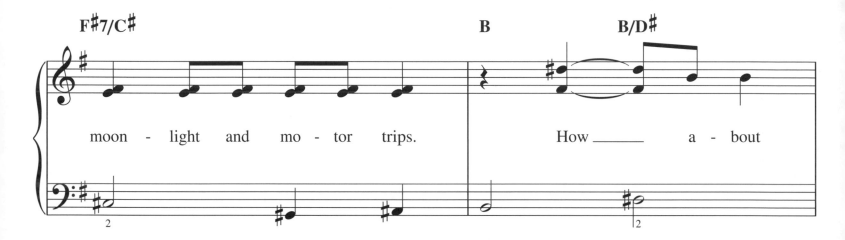

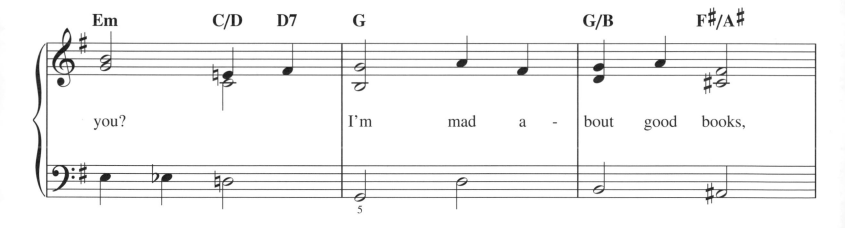

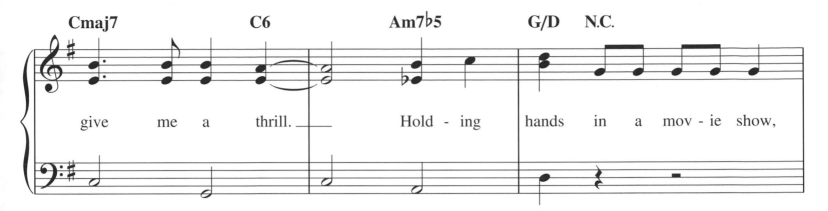

give me a thrill. ___ Hold - ing hands in a mov - ie show,

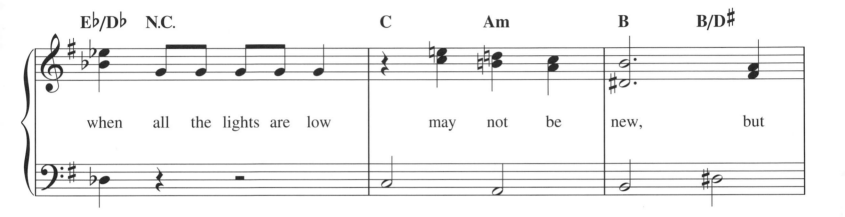

when all the lights are low may not be new, but

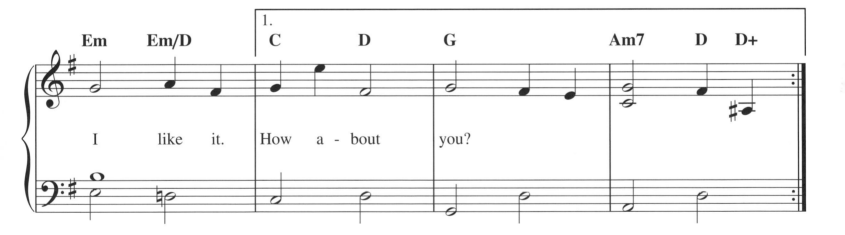

I like it. How a - bout you?

How a - bout you?

rit. *molto rit.*

IF YOU COULD SEE ME NOW

Lyric by CARL SIGMAN
Music by TADD DAMERON

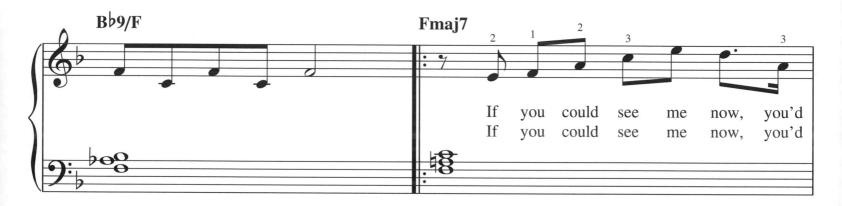

If you could see me now, you'd
If you could see me now, you'd

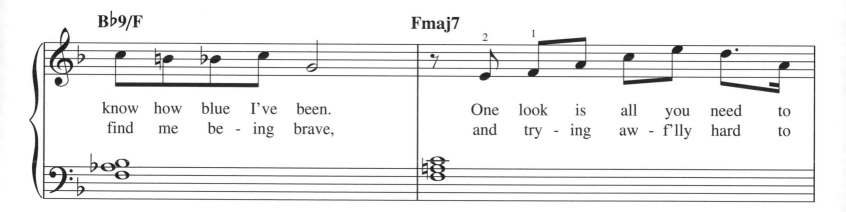

know how blue I've been.
find me be-ing brave,

One look is all you need to
and try-ing aw-f'lly hard to

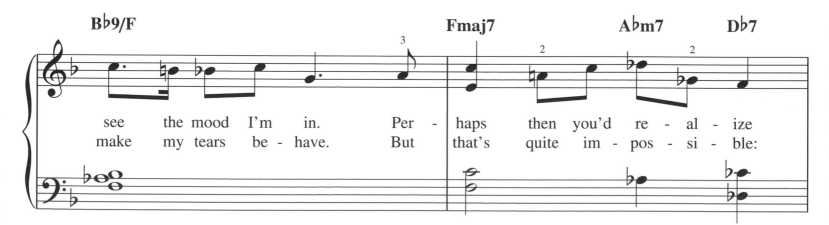

see the mood I'm in.
make my tears be-have.

Per - haps then you'd re-al-ize
But that's quite im-pos-si-ble:

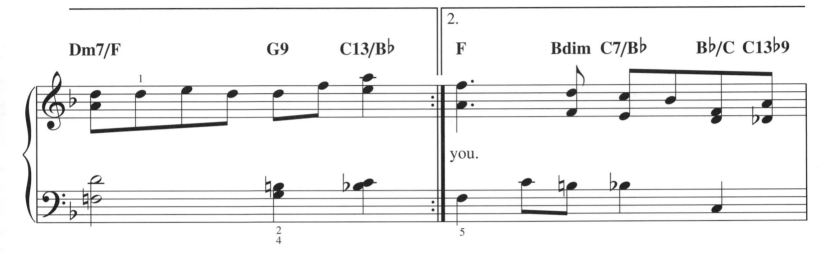

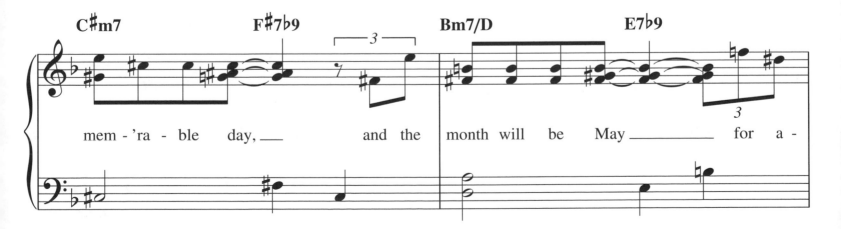

60

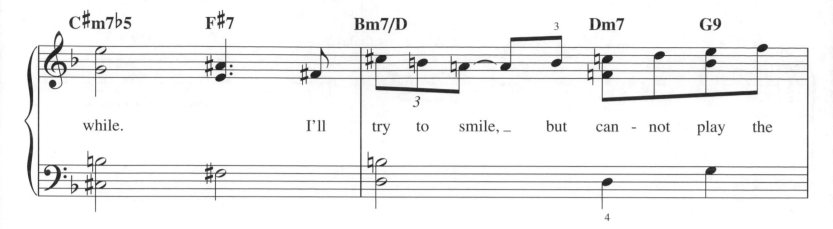

while. I'll try to smile, _ but can - not play the

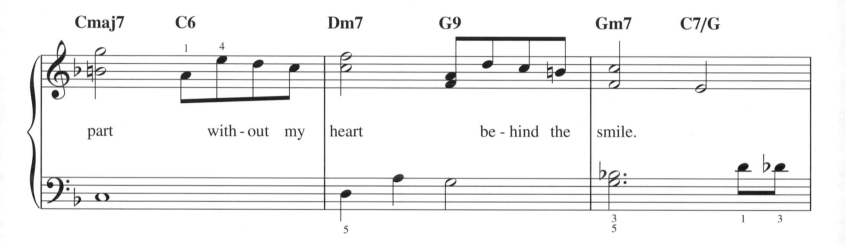

part with - out my heart be - hind the smile.

The way I feel for you, I nev - er could dis - guise. _

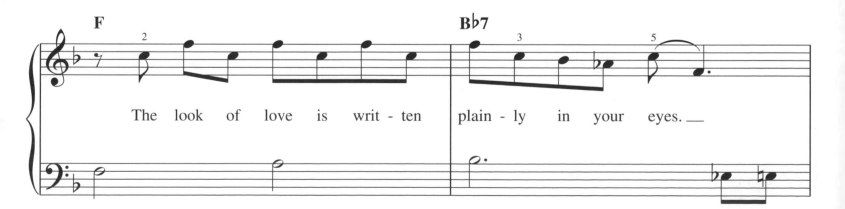

The look of love is writ - ten plain - ly in your eyes. _

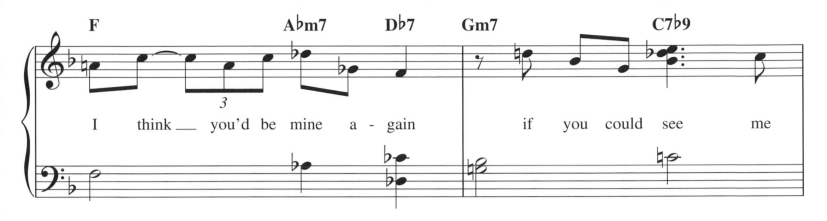

I think ___ you'd be mine a - gain if you could see me

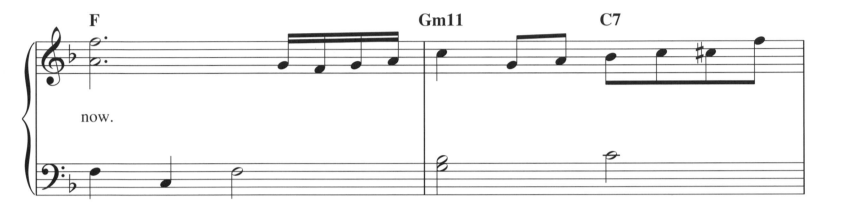

now.

You would be mine if you could

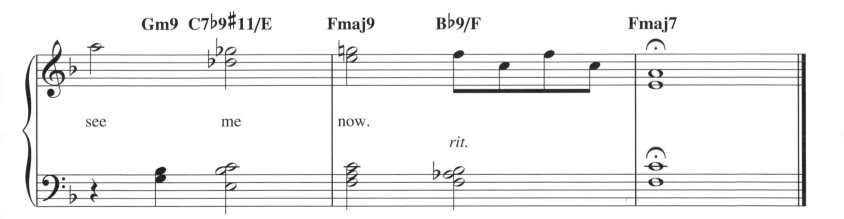

see me now.

IN YOUR OWN SWEET WAY

By DAVE BRUBECK

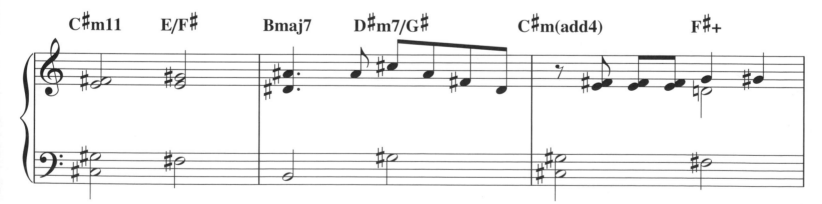

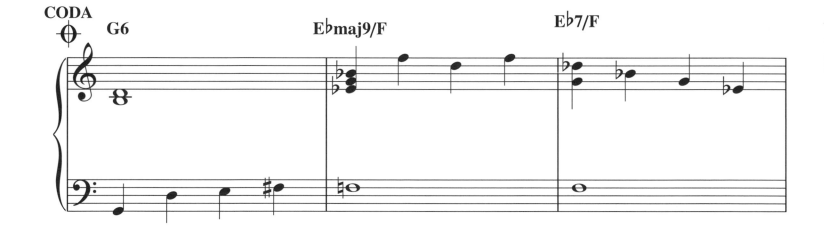

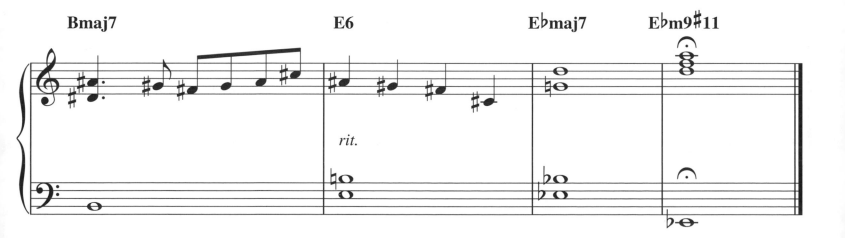

IT'S YOU OR NO ONE

from the Film ROMANCE ON THE HIGH SEAS

Words by SAMMY CAHN
Music by JULE STYNE

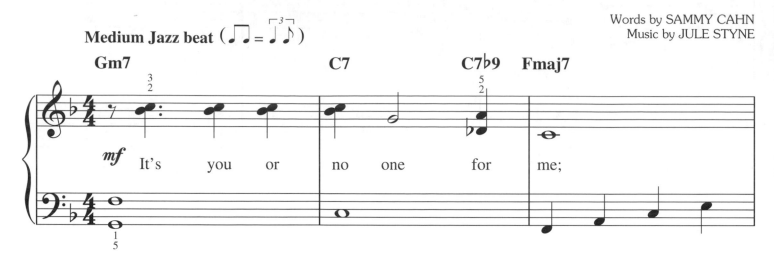

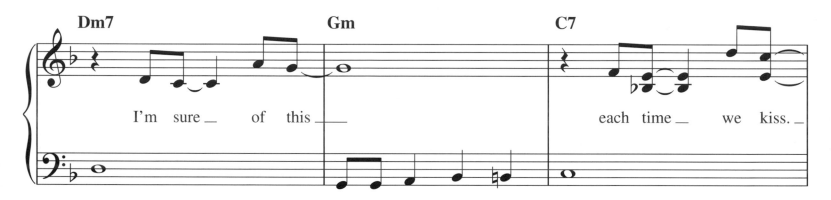

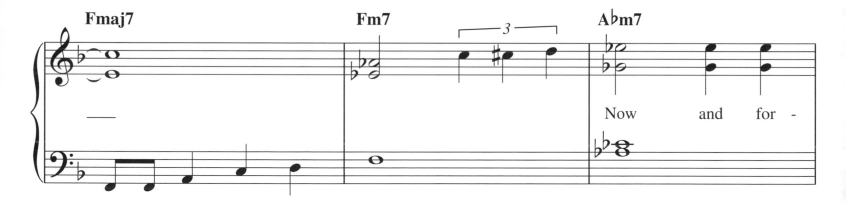

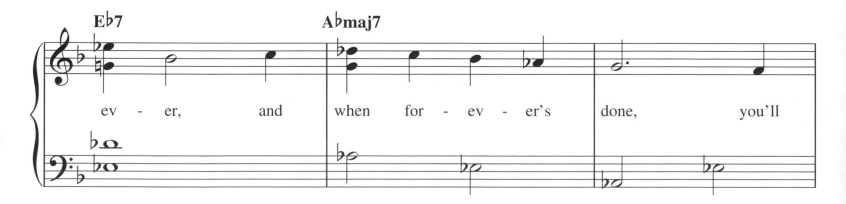

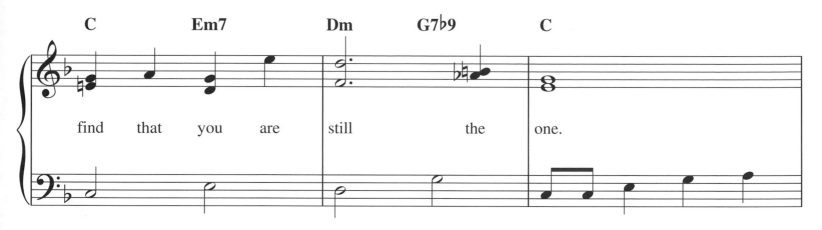

C   Em7   Dm   G7♭9   C

find that you are still the one.

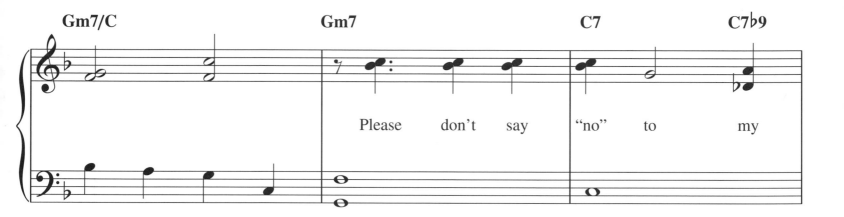

Gm7/C   Gm7   C7   C7♭9

Please don't say "no" to my

Fmaj7   Dm7   Gm

plea, 'cause if ___ you do, ___

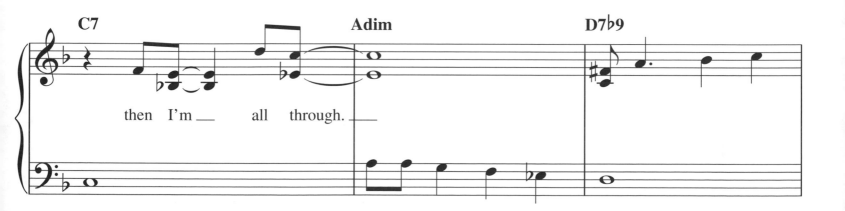

C7   Adim   D7♭9

then I'm ___ all through. ___

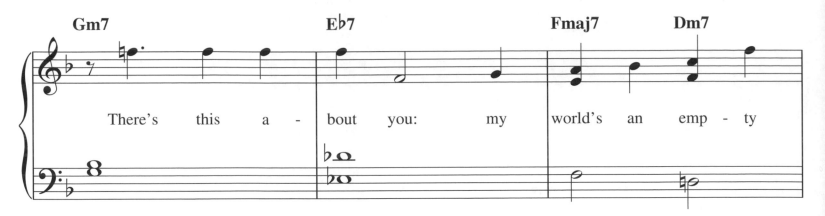

There's this a - bout you: my world's an emp - ty

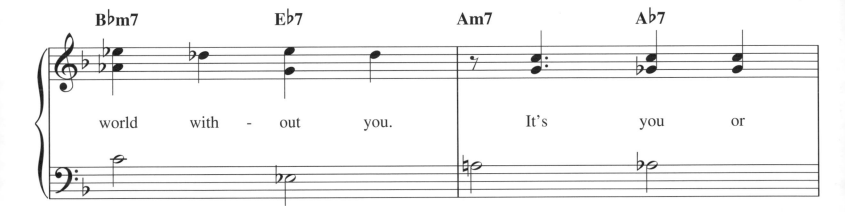

world with - out you. It's you or

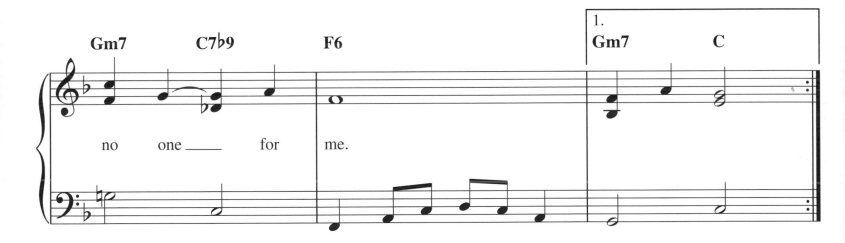

no one ___ for me.

1.

2.

THE LAMP IS LOW

Music by PETER DeROSE and BERT SHEFTER
Words by MITCHELL PARISH
Original French Lyrics by YVETTE BARUCH
Melody based on a Theme from Ravel's PAVANE

Slowly, with much expression

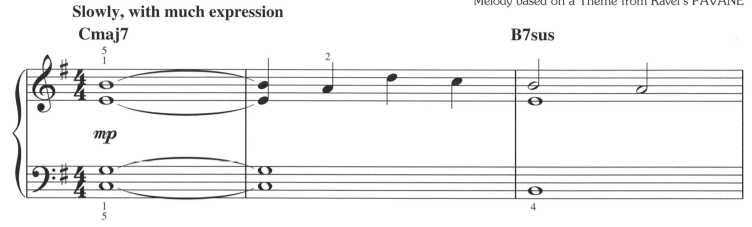

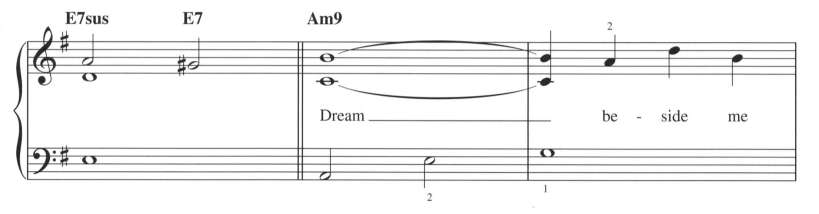

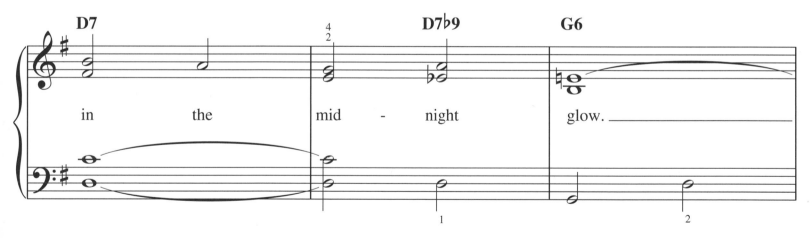

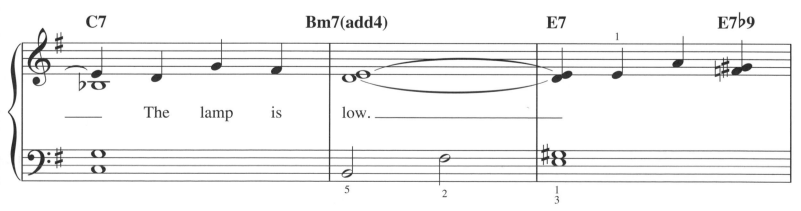

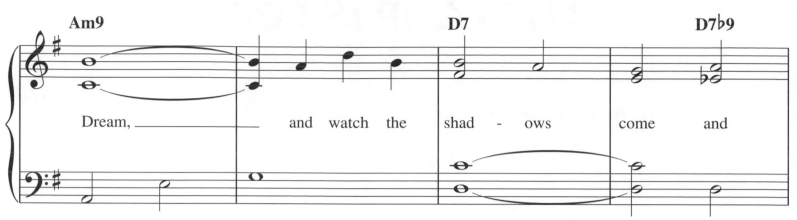

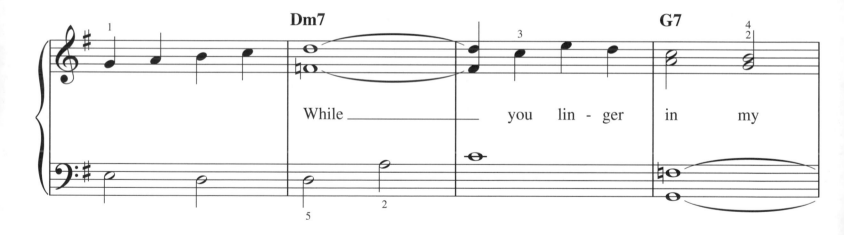

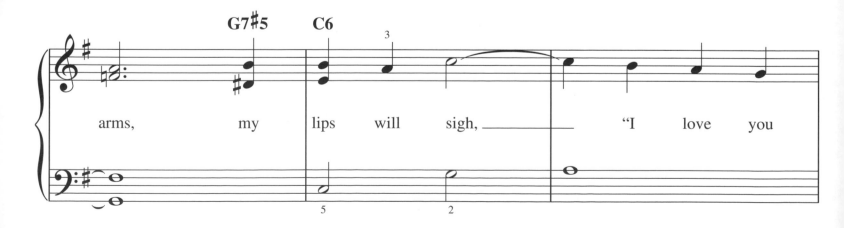

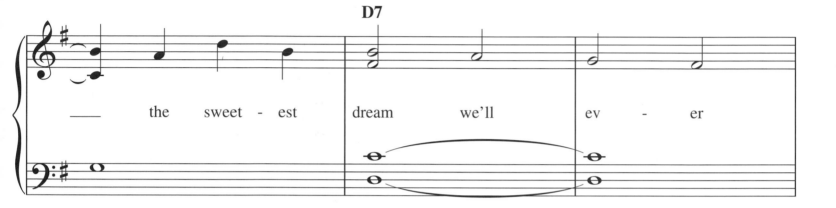

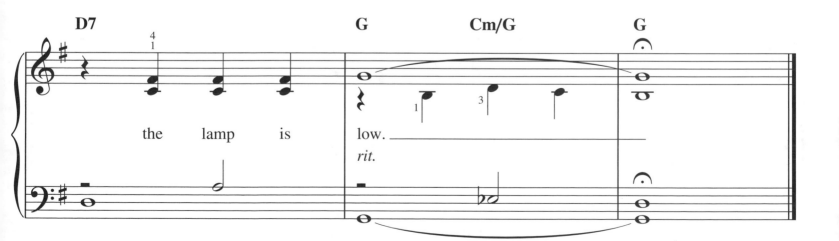

JUMPIN' AT THE WOODSIDE

Music by COUNT BASIE
Words by JON HENDRICKS

Bright Bounce

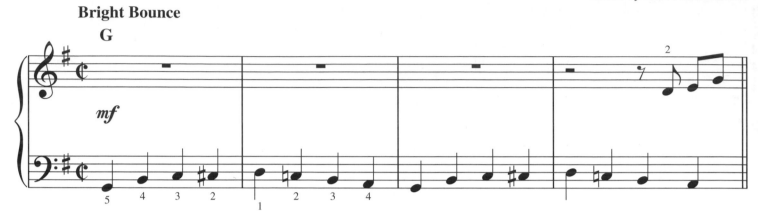

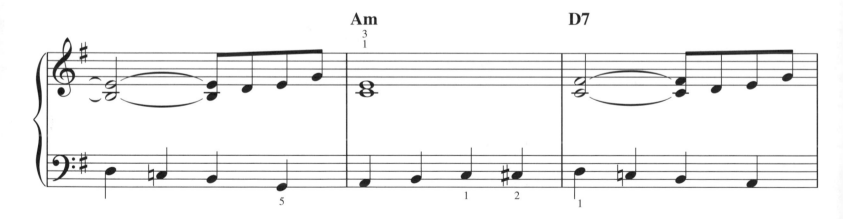

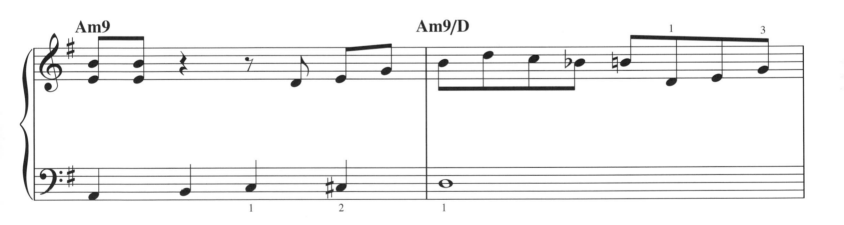

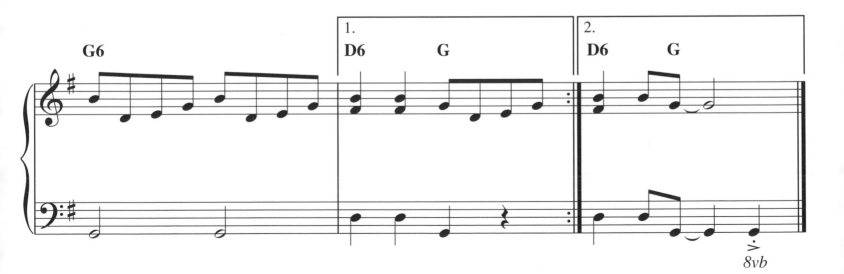

JUST FRIENDS

Lyrics by SAM M. LEWIS
Music by JOHN KLENNER

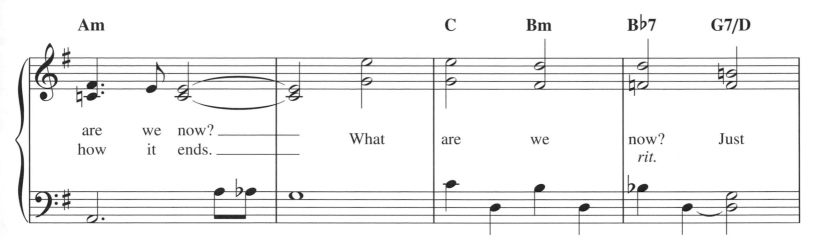

Am ... **C** **Bm** **Bb7** **G7/D**

are   we   now? _____ What   are   we   now?   Just
how   it   ends. _____   *rit.*

With a lilt (♩♪ = ⌐3⌐ ♩♪)

Cmaj7 ⌐ 3 ⌐ **Cm6**

friends, _____   lov - ers   no   more; _____

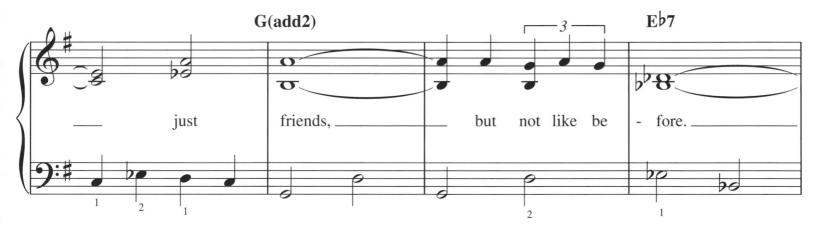

G(add2) ⌐ 3 ⌐ **Eb7**

_____ just   friends, _____ but   not   like   be - fore. _____

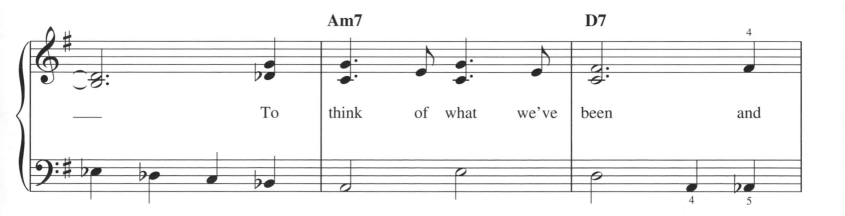

Am7 **D7**

_____ To   think   of   what   we've   been   and

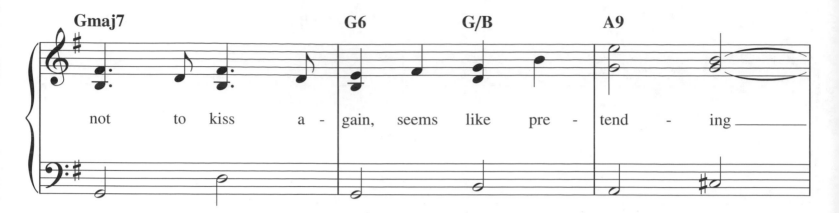

Gmaj7　　　　　**G6**　　**G/B**　　**A9**

not　　to　kiss　a - gain,　seems　like　pre - tend - ing _____

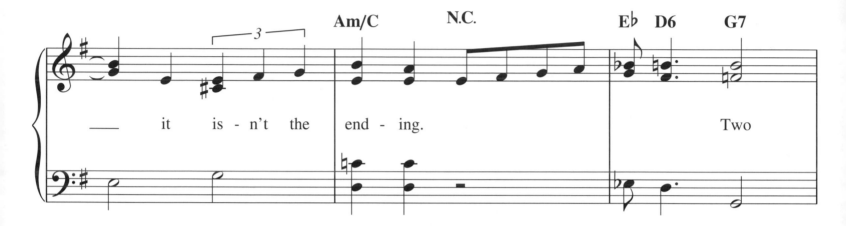

Am/C　　**N.C.**　　**E♭**　**D6**　**G7**

_____　it　is - n't　the　end - ing.　　　　　　Two

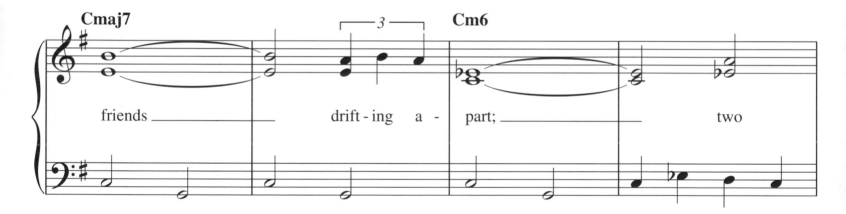

Cmaj7　　　　　**Cm6**

friends _____　drift - ing　a - part; _____　two

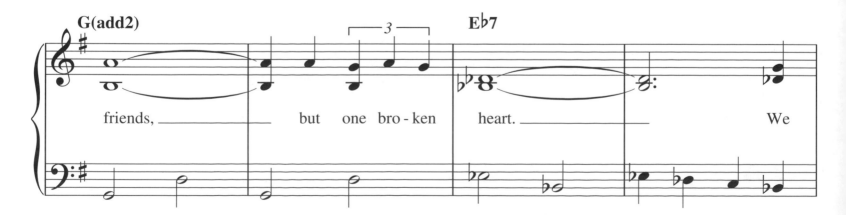

G(add2)　　　　**E♭7**

friends, _____　but　one　bro - ken　heart. _____　We

loved, we laughed, we cried, and sud-den-ly love died. The sto-ry

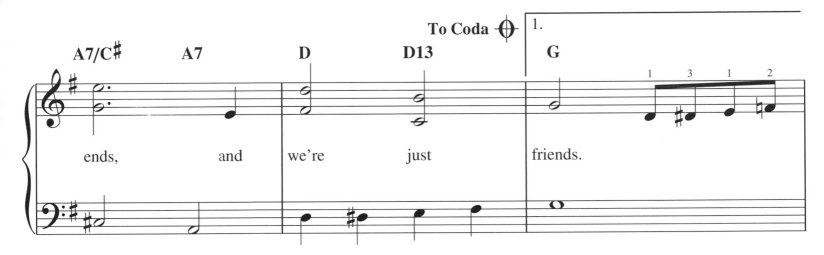

ends, and we're just friends.

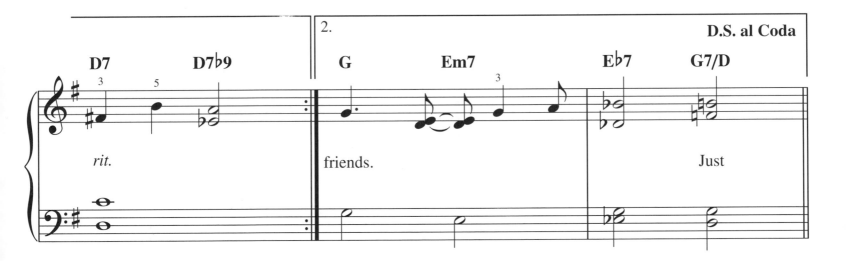

rit. friends. Just

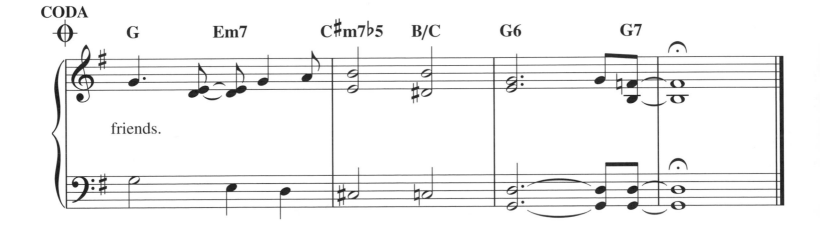

friends.

LAURA

Lyrics by JOHNNY MERCER
Music by DAVID RAKSIN

Slowly, with expression

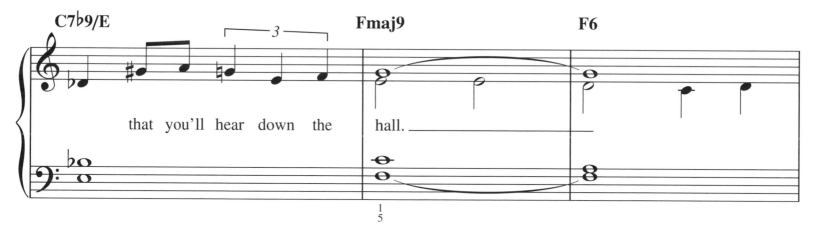

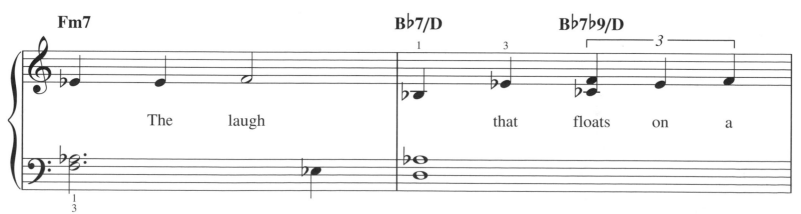

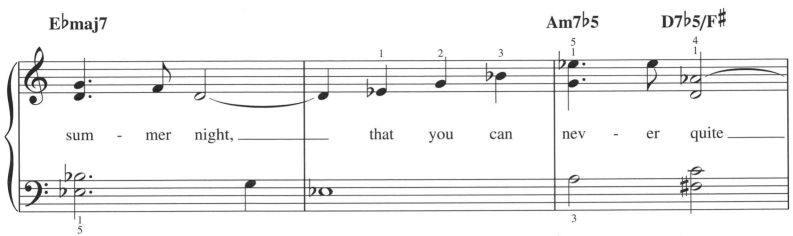

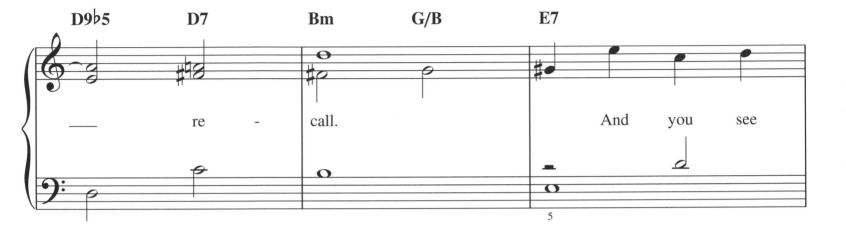

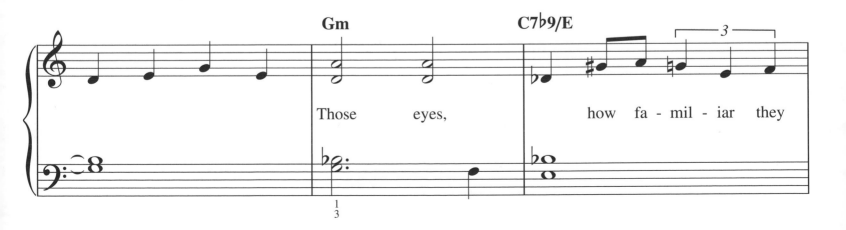

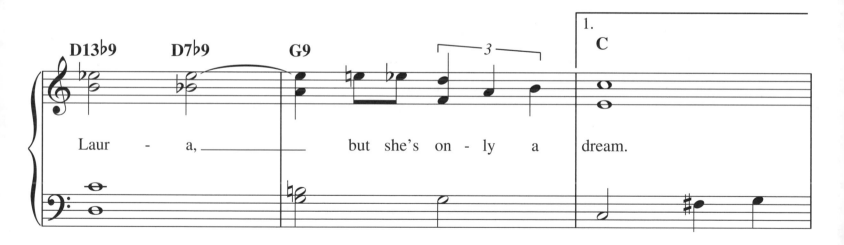

MINNIE THE MOOCHER

Words and Music by CAB CALLOWAY
and IRVING MILLS

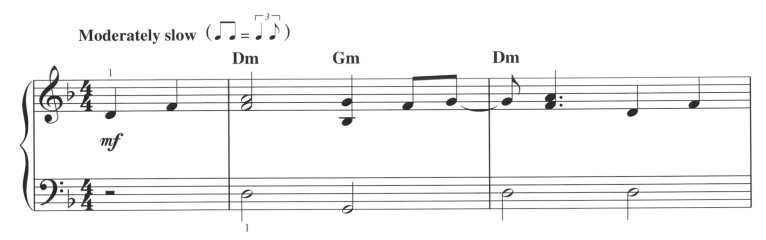

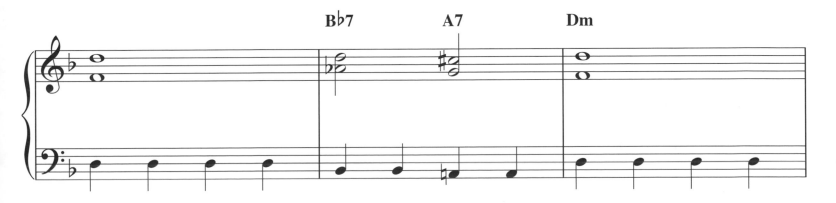

Bb7 A7 Dm

Hey, folks, here's a sto - ry of Min - nie the Mooch - er;
She messed a - round with a bloke _ named Smok - ey.

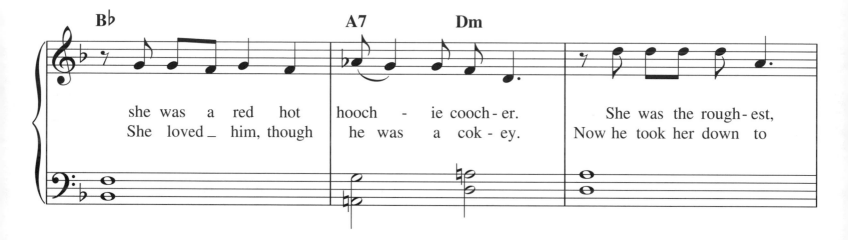

Bb A7 Dm

she was a red hot hooch - ie cooch - er. She was the rough - est,
She loved _ him, though he was a cok - ey. Now he took her down to

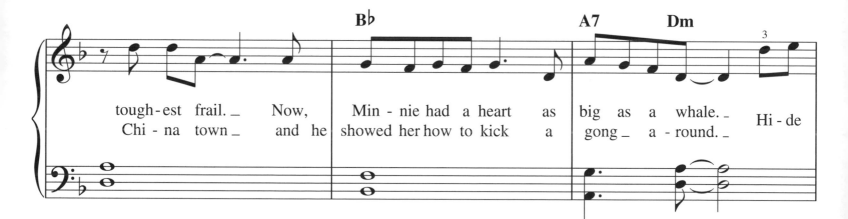

Bb A7 Dm

tough - est frail. _ Now, Min - nie had a heart as big as a whale. _ Hi - de
Chi - na town _ and he showed her how to kick a gong _ a - round. _

hi - de hi - de hi. (Hi - de hi - de hi - de hi.) Ho - de ho - de ho - de ho. (Ho - de

ho - de ho - de ho.) He - de he - de he - de he. (He - de he - de he - de he.) Hi - de

A   Dm   A   Dm

hi - de hi - de hi. (Hi - de hi - de hi - de hi.)

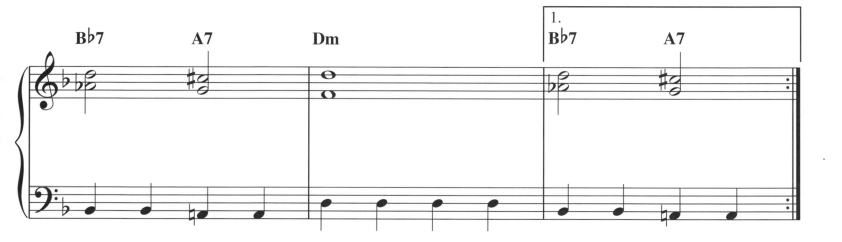

B♭7   A7   Dm   1. B♭7   A7

2. B♭7   A7   Dm

Now she had a dream_ a - bout a king from Swe - den.

He gave her things that she __ was need - in'. Now he built her a home __ of

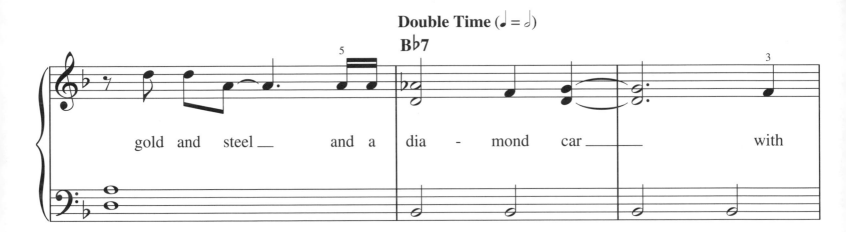

Double Time ($\textit{♩} = \textit{♪}$)

gold and steel __ and a dia - mond car __ with

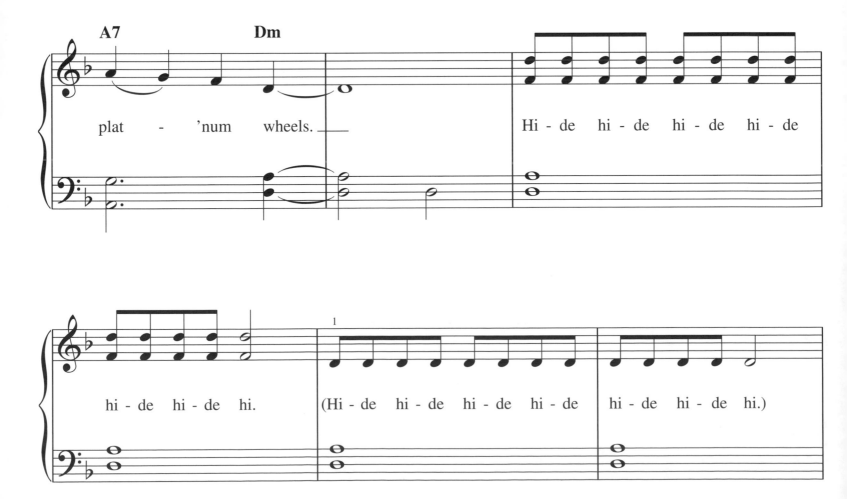

plat - 'num wheels. __ Hi - de hi - de hi - de hi - de

hi - de hi - de hi. (Hi - de hi - de hi - de hi - de hi - de hi - de hi.)

Ho - de ho - de ho - de ho - de   ho - de ho - de ho.   (Ho - de ho - de ho - de ho - de

ho - de ho - de ho.)   He - de he - de he - de he - de   he - de he - de he.

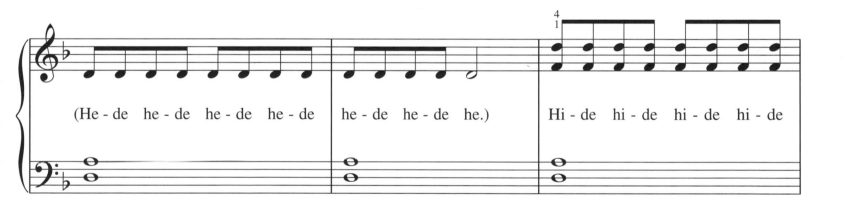

(He - de he - de he - de he - de   he - de he - de he.)   Hi - de hi - de hi - de hi - de

hi - de hi - de hi.   (Hi - de hi - de hi - de hi - de   hi - de hi - de hi.)

84

gave her his town-house and his rac - ing hors - es. Each meal she ate was a

doz - en cours - es. She had a mil-lion dol-lars in nick-els and dimes, _ she

sat a-round and count-ed one mil - lion times._ Hi - de hi-de hi-de hi. (Hi - de

hi - de - hi - de hi.) Ho - de ho - de ho - de ho. (Ho - de ho - de ho - de ho.) He - de

he - de he - de he. (He - de he - de he - de he.) Hi - de hi - de hi - de hi. (Hi - de

Much slower

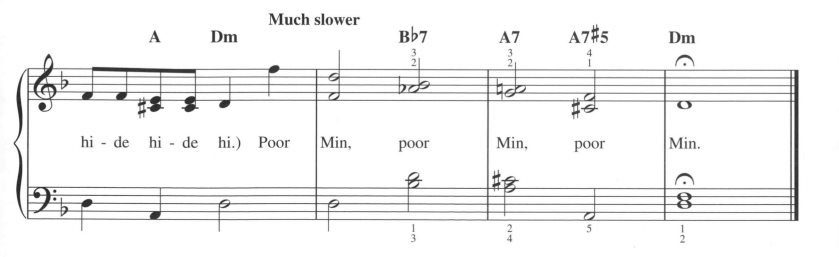

hi - de hi - de hi.) Poor Min, poor Min, poor Min.

LI'L DARLIN'

By NEAL HEFTI

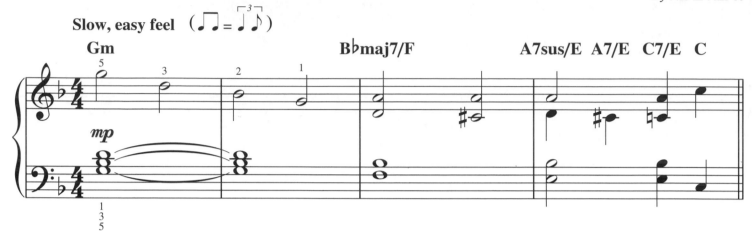

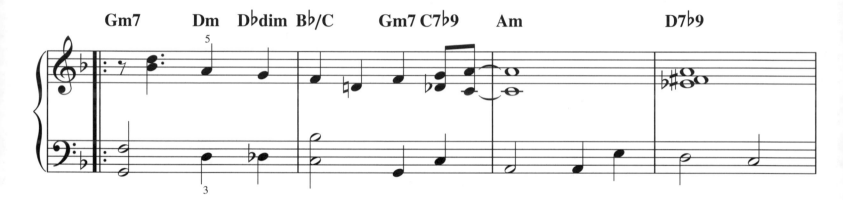

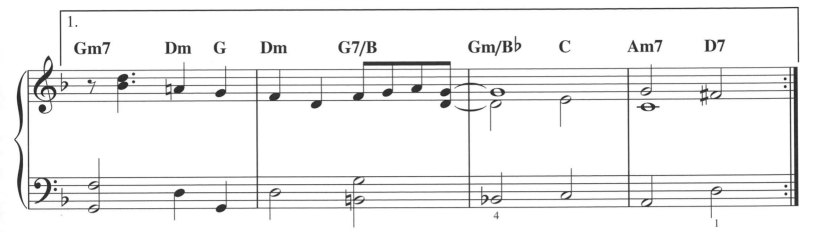

LOVE FOR SALE
from THE NEW YORKERS

Words and Music by
COLE PORTER

Lively Latin feel

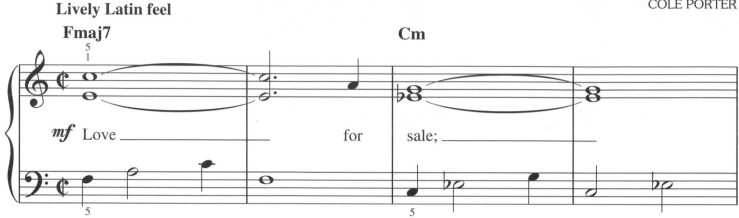

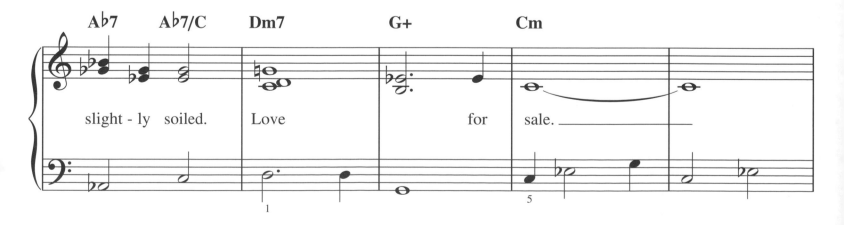

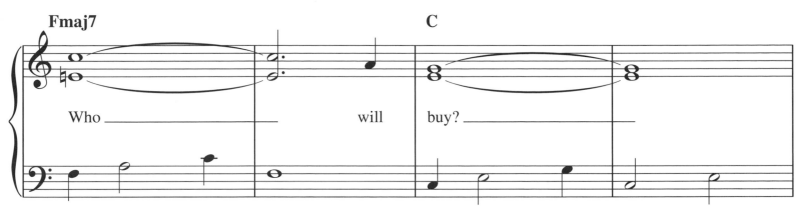

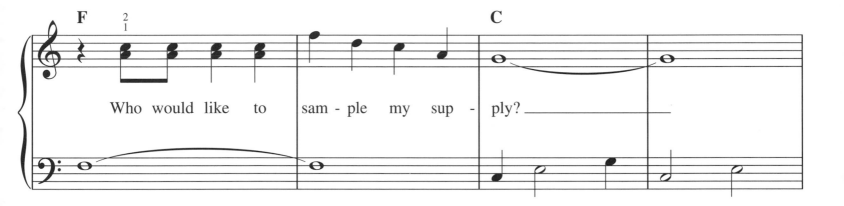

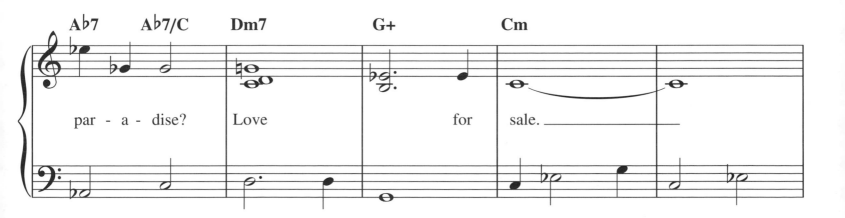

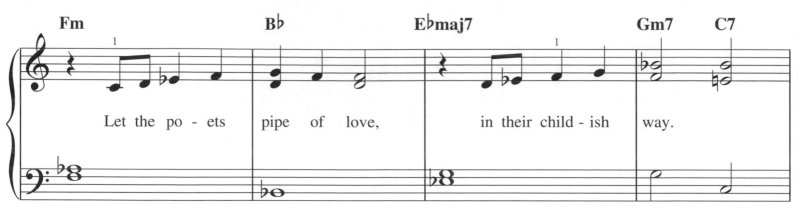

Let the po - ets pipe of love, in their child - ish way.

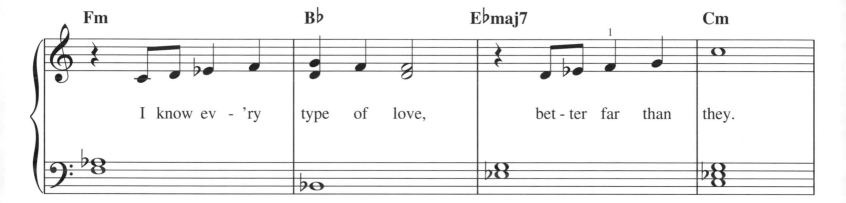

I know ev - 'ry type of love, bet - ter far than they.

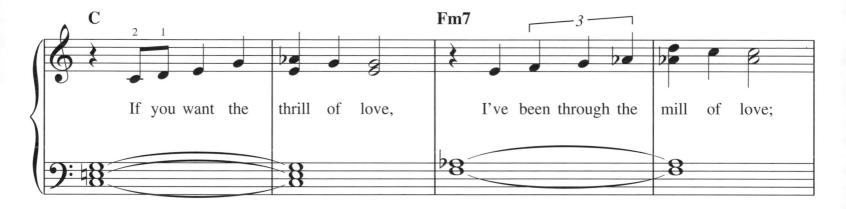

If you want the thrill of love, I've been through the mill of love;

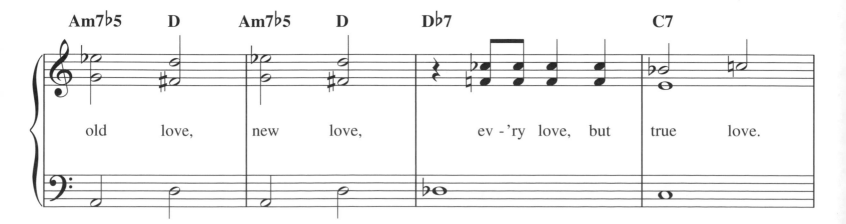

old love, new love, ev - 'ry love, but true love.

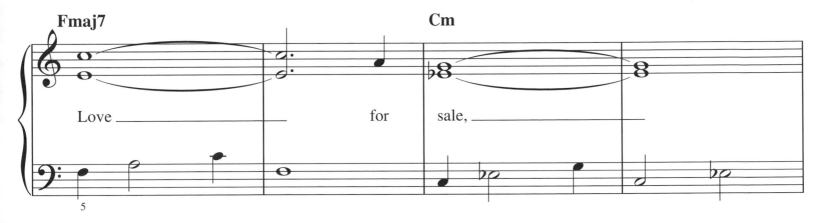

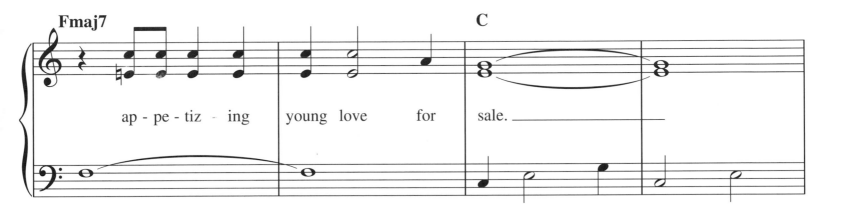

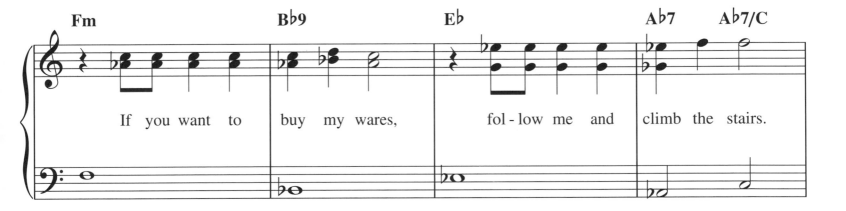

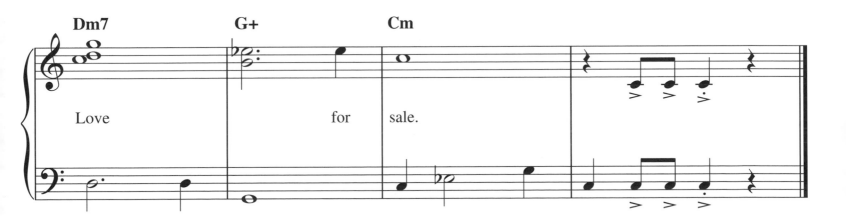

MACK THE KNIFE
from THE THREEPENNY OPERA

English Words by MARC BLITZSTEIN
Original German Words by BERT BRECHT
Music by KURT WEILL

Moderately

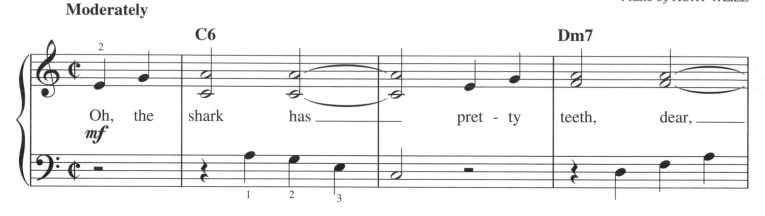

Oh, the shark has _____ pret-ty teeth, dear, _____

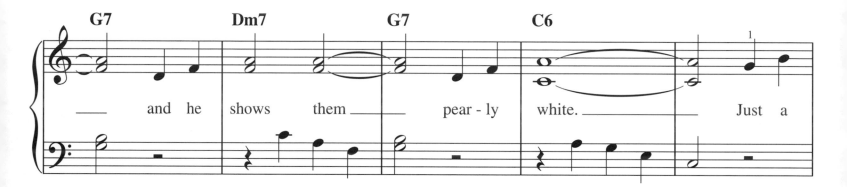

_____ and he shows them _____ pear-ly white. _____ Just a

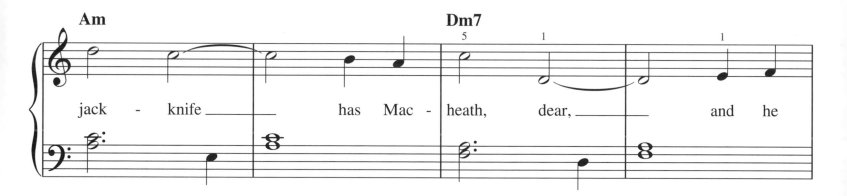

jack - knife _____ has Mac - heath, dear, _____ and he

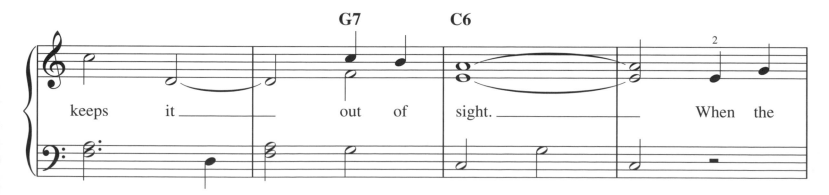

keeps it _____ out of sight. _____ When the

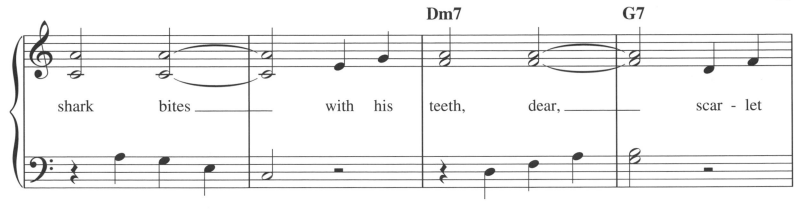

shark   bites _____   with his teeth, dear, _____   scar - let

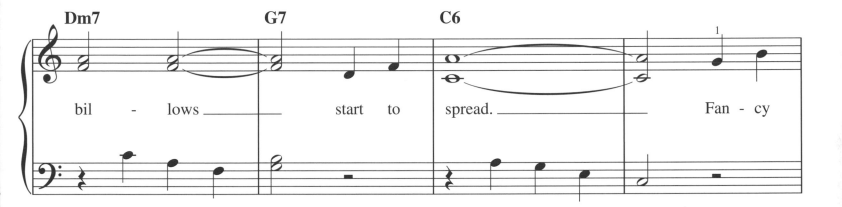

bil - lows _____   start to spread. _____   Fan - cy

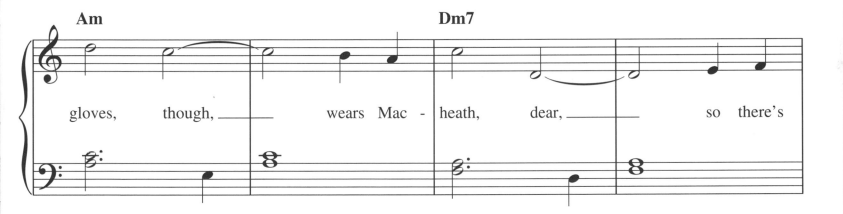

gloves,   though, _____   wears Mac - heath,   dear, _____   so there's

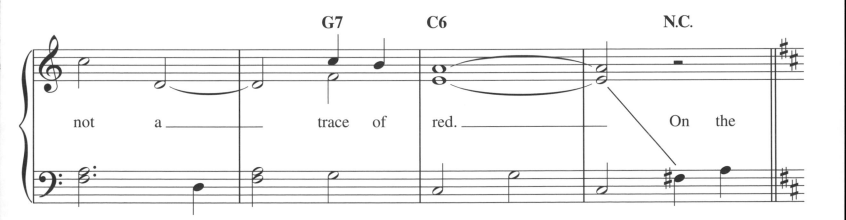

not   a _____   trace of red. _____   On the

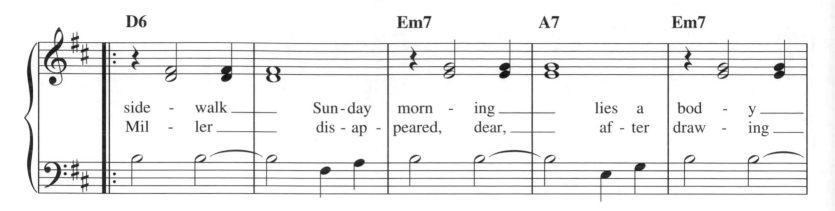

D6 **Em7** **A7** **Em7**

side - walk ____ Sun - day morn - ing ____ lies a bod - y ____
Mil - ler ____ dis - ap - peared, dear, ____ af - ter draw - ing ____

A7 **D6** **Bm**

____ ooz - ing life: ____ some-one's sneak - ing ____ 'round the
____ out his cash; ____ and Mac - heath spends ____ like a

Em7 **A7**

cor - ner, ____ is the some - one ____ Mack the
sail - or, ____ did our boy do ____ some - thing

D6

Knife? ____ From a tug - boat ____ by the
rash? ____ Su - key Taw - dry, ____ Jen - ny

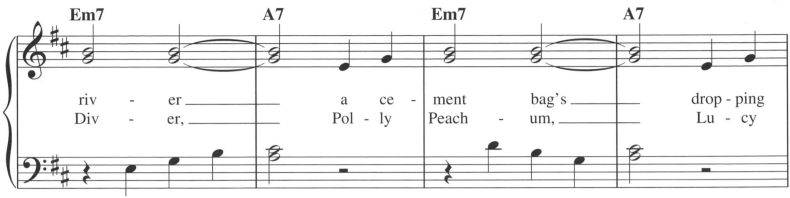

riv - er _____ a ce - ment bag's _____ drop - ping
Div - er, _____ Pol - ly Peach - um, _____ Lu - cy

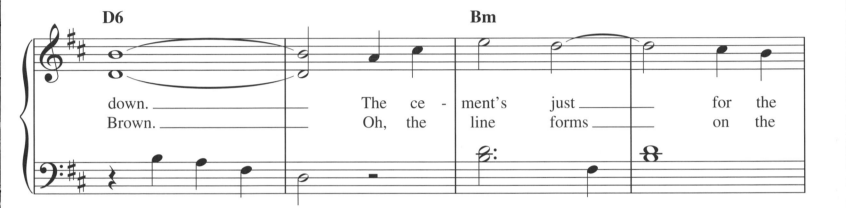

down. _____ The ce - ment's just _____ for the
Brown. _____ Oh, the line forms _____ on the

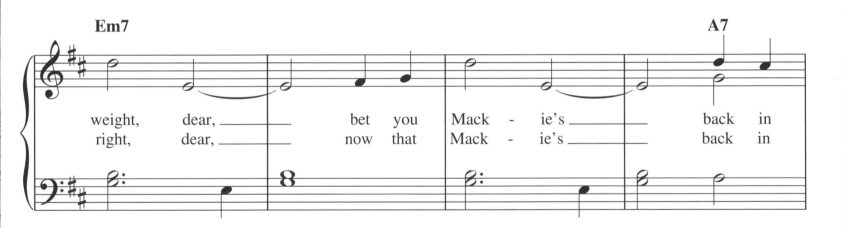

weight, dear, _____ bet you Mack - ie's _____ back in
right, dear, _____ now that Mack - ie's _____ back in

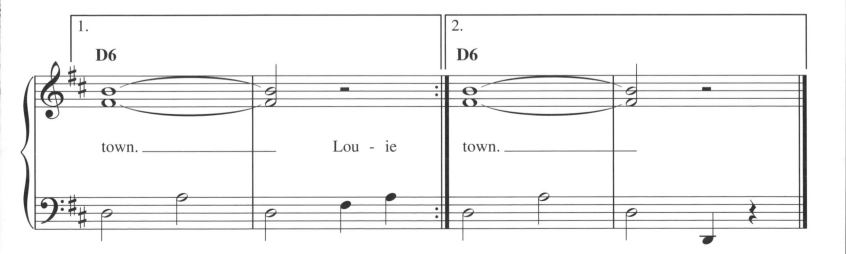

1.
D6
town. _____ Lou - ie

2.
D6
town. _____

THE MORE I SEE YOU

from the Twentieth Century-Fox Technicolor Musical BILLY ROSE'S DIAMOND HORSESHOES

Words by MACK GORDON
Music by HARRY WARREN

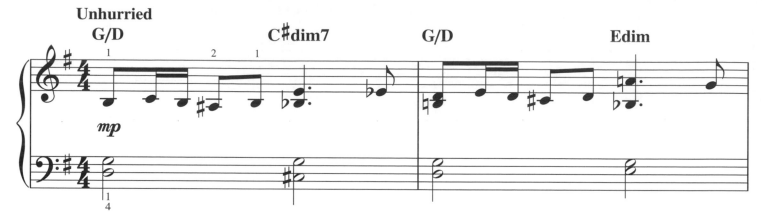

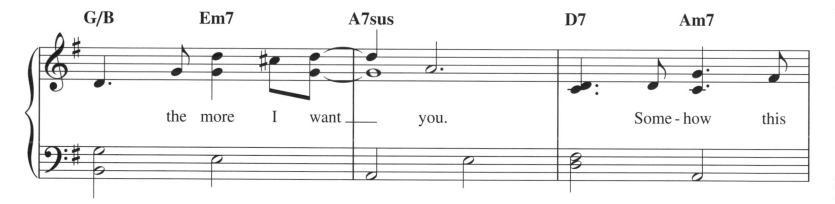

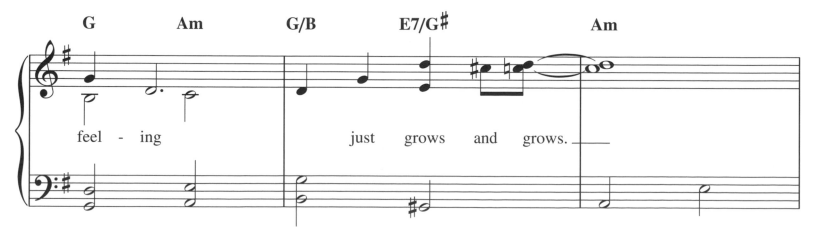

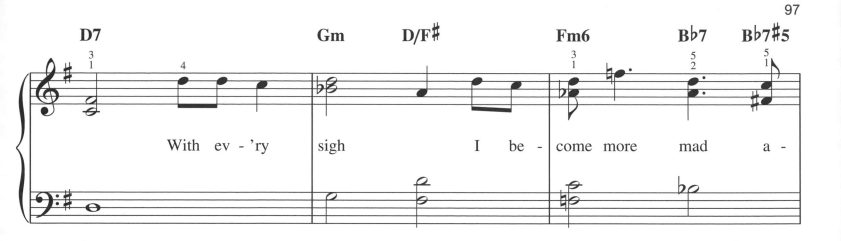

With ev - 'ry sigh I be - come more mad a -

bout you, more lost with - out you, and so it goes.

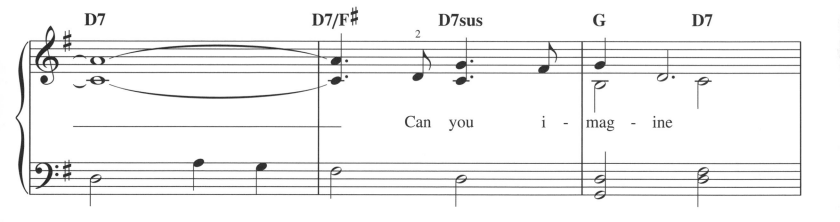

Can you i - mag - ine

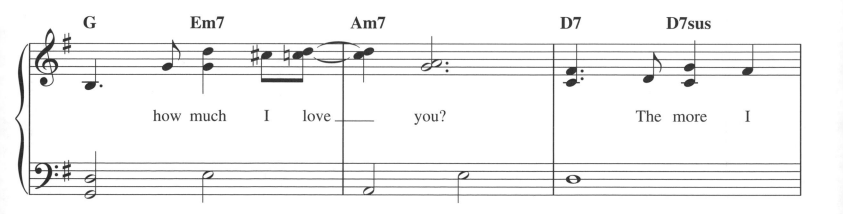

how much I love _____ you? The more I

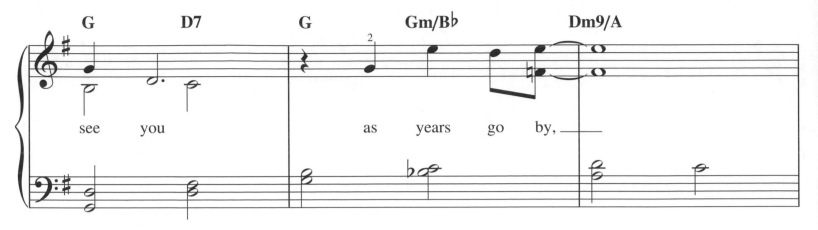

see   you   as years go   by, ____

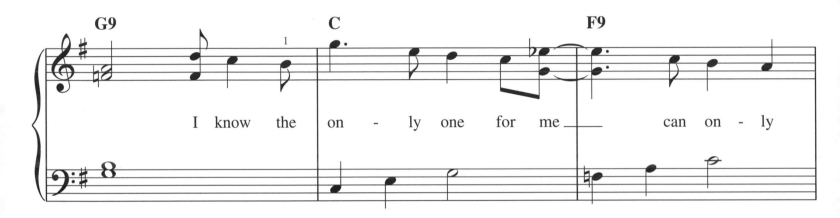

I   know   the   on - ly one for me ____   can on - ly

be   you.   My arms won't   free   you,   and my heart won't

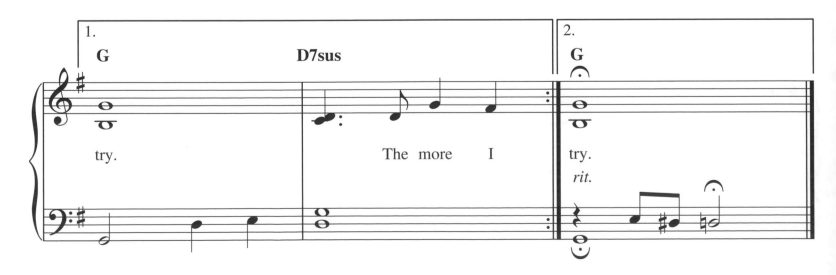

1.
try.   The more   I

2.
try.
rit.

NUAGES

By DJANGO REINHARDT
and JACQUES LARUE

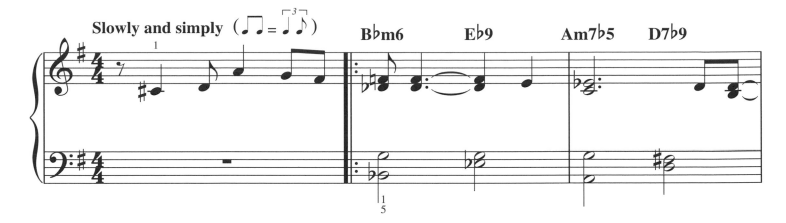

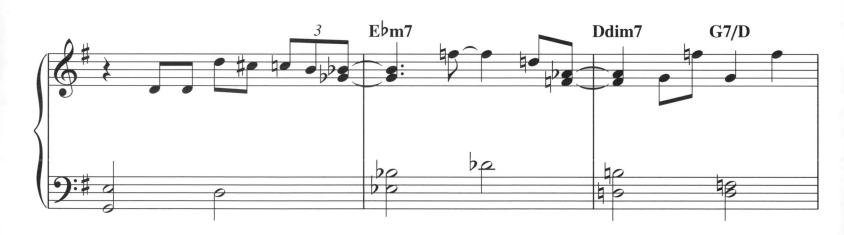

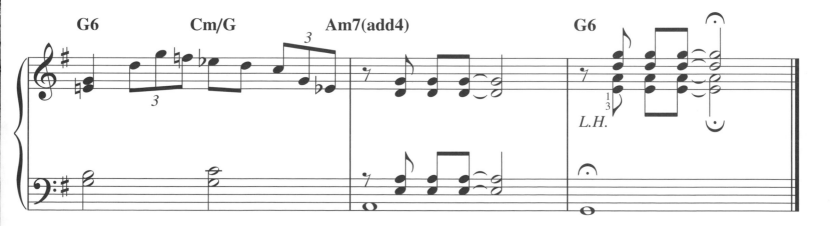

THEME FROM "NEW YORK, NEW YORK"

from NEW YORK, NEW YORK

Words by FRED EBB
Music by JOHN KANDER

Start spread-in' the news, I'm leav-ing to-

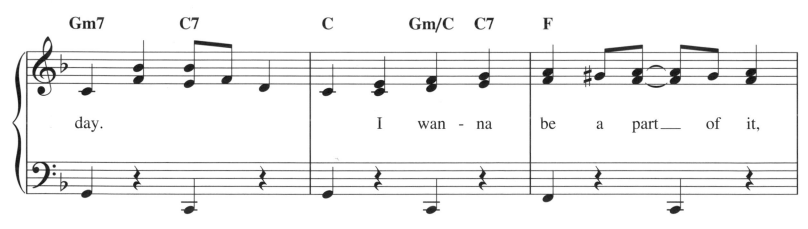

day. I wan-na be a part___ of it,

New York, New York. These vag-a-bond

shoes _____ are long - ing to stray

and step a - round the heart __ of it,   New York, New
(D.S.) *Instrumental*

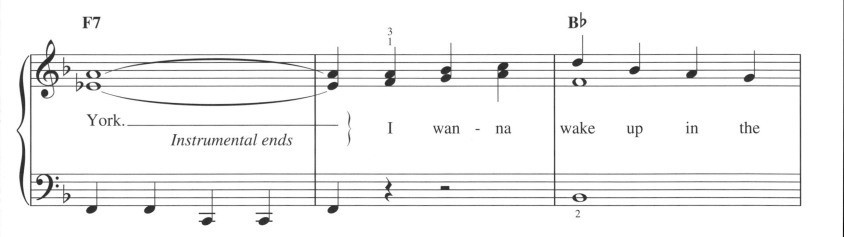

York. _____   I wan - na wake up in the
Instrumental ends

To Coda ⊕

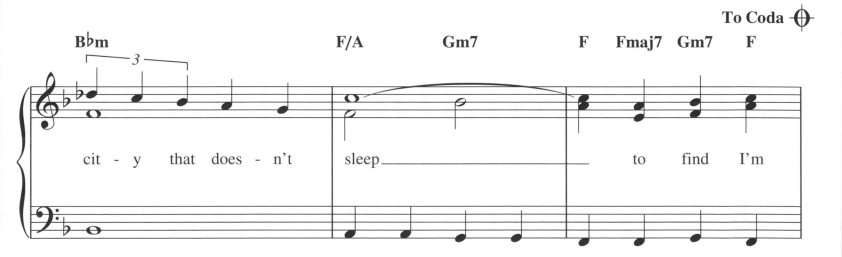

cit - y that does - n't   sleep _____ to find I'm

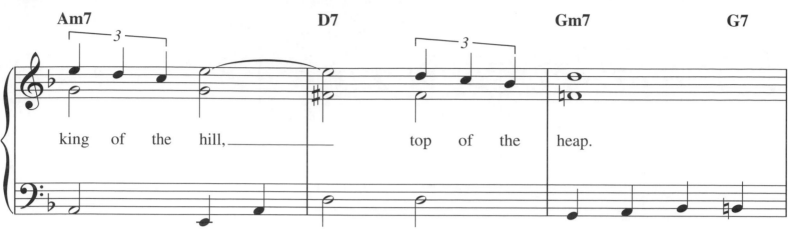

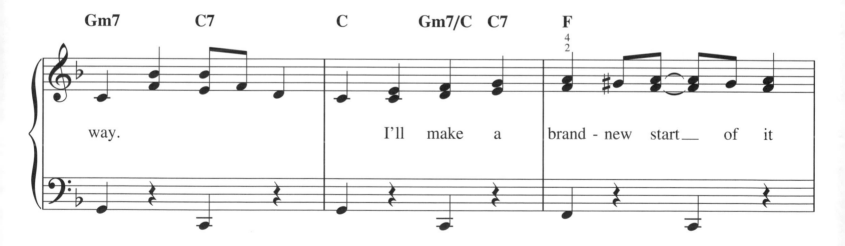

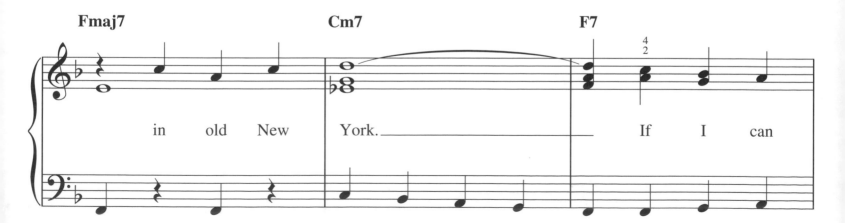

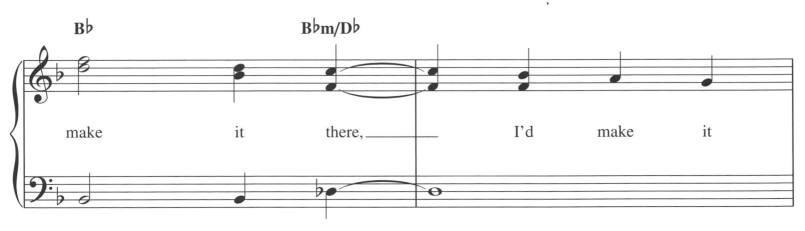

make it there, ____ I'd make it

an - y - where. ____ It's up to

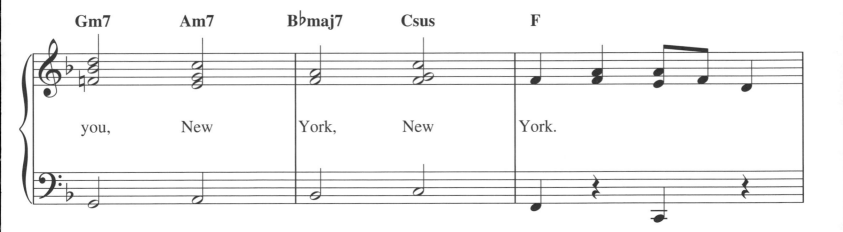

you, New York, New York.

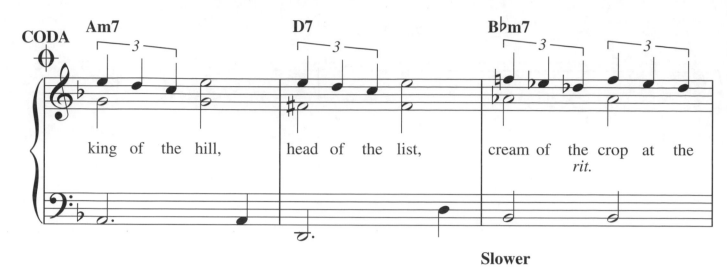

king of the hill, head of the list, cream of the crop at the

top of the heap. My lit - tle town blues

_are melt - ing a - way. I'll make a

brand - new start of it in old New York.

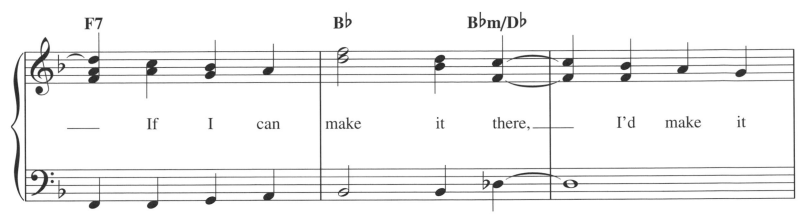

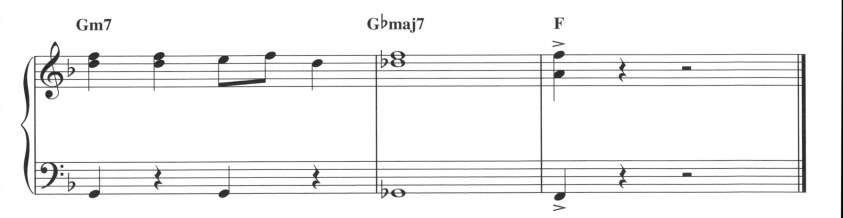

NIGHT AND DAY

Words and Music by
COLE PORTER

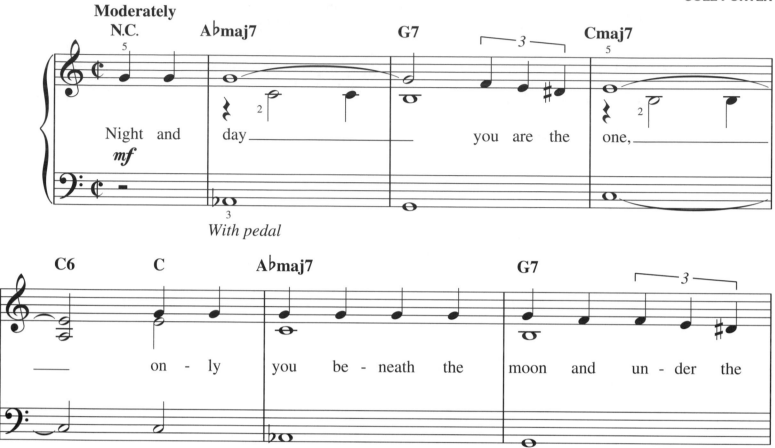

Night and day ___ you are the one, ___

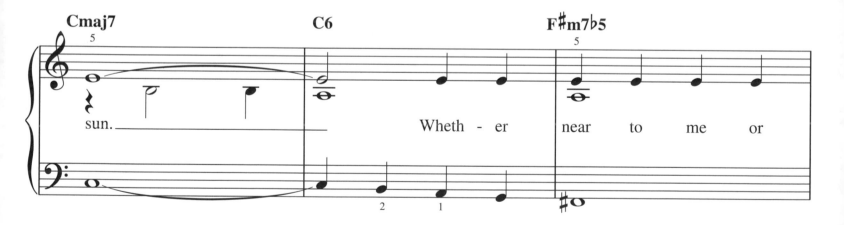

___ on - ly you be - neath the moon and un - der the

sun. ___ Wheth - er near to me or

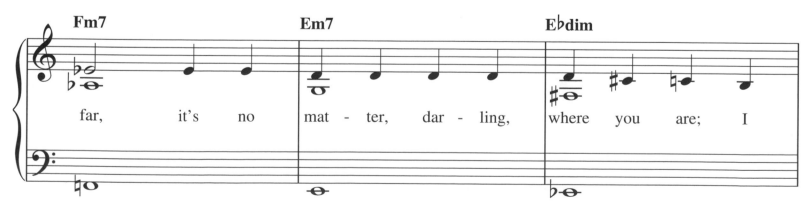

far, it's no mat - ter, dar - ling, where you are; I

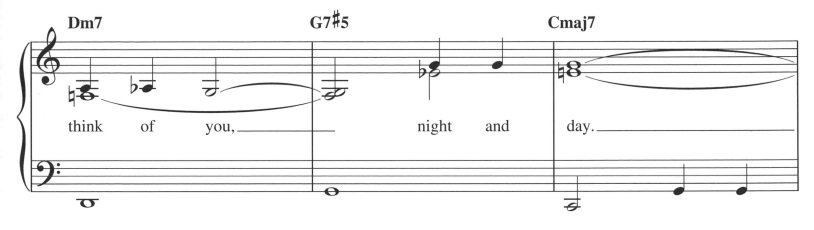

think of you,_____ night and day._____

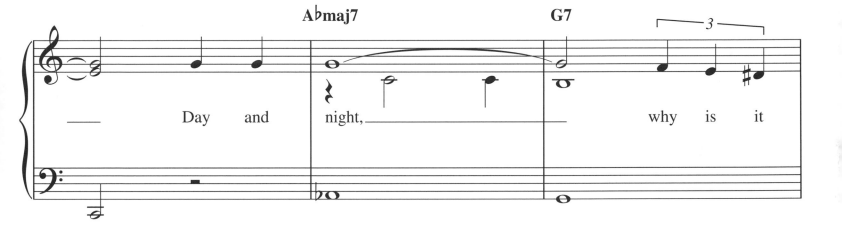

_____ Day and night,_____ why is it

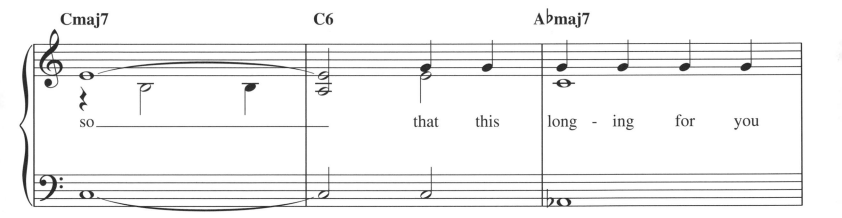

so_____ that this long - ing for you

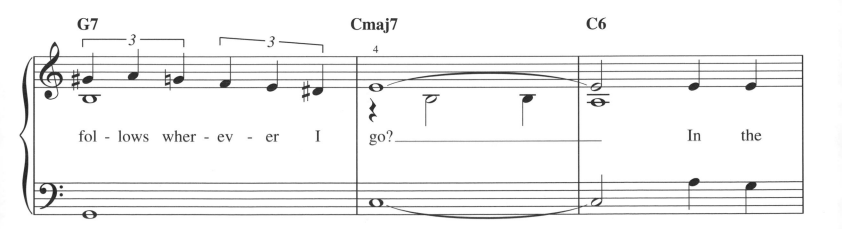

fol - lows wher - ev - er I go?_____ In the

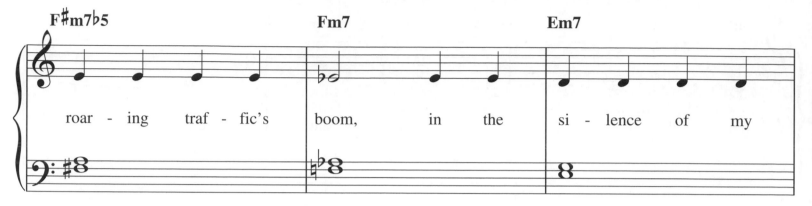

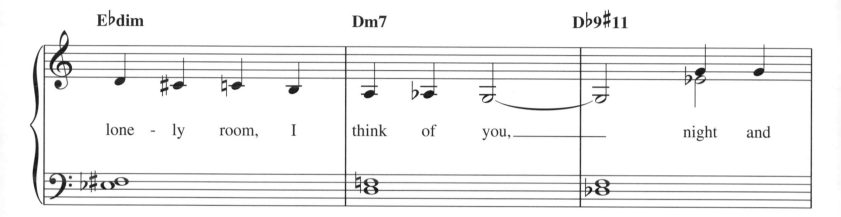

oh, such a hun - gry yearn - ing burn - ing in - side of me.___

___ And its tor - ment won't be through 'til you

let me spend my life mak - ing love to you day and night,___

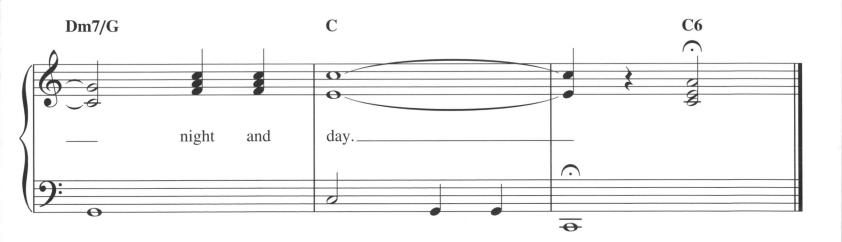

___ night and day.___

ON GREEN DOLPHIN STREET

Lyrics by NED WASHINGTON
Music by BRONISLAU KAPER

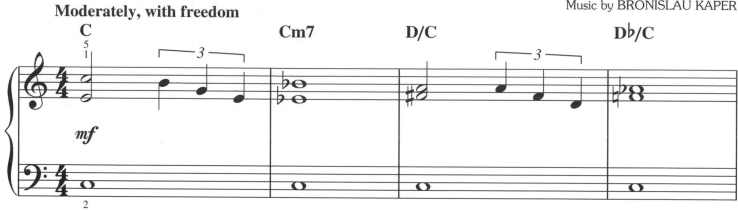

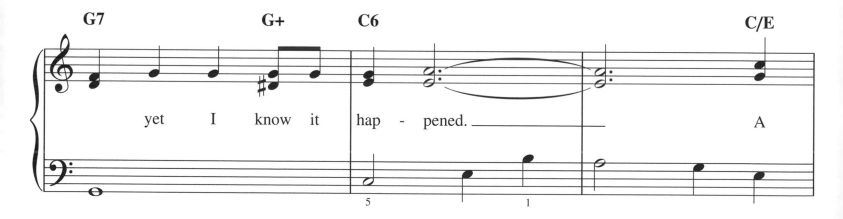

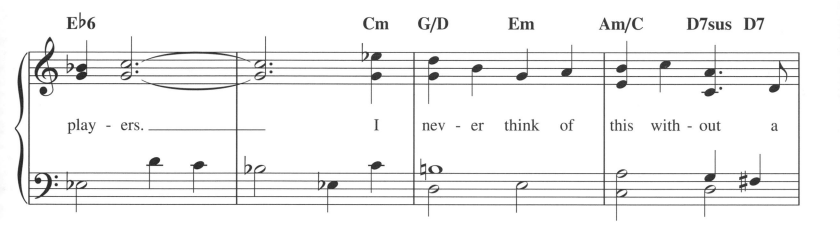

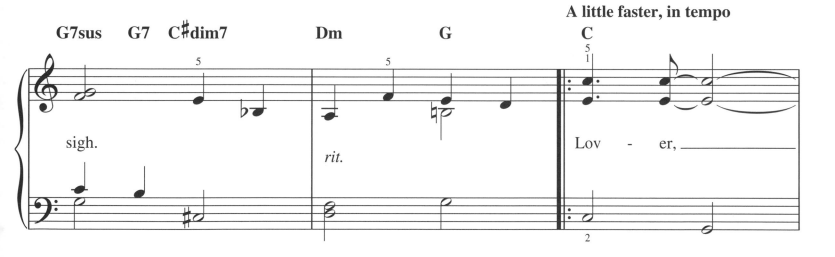

planning to stay. Green Dol - phin

Street sup - plied the set - ting, the set - ting for

nights be - yond for - get - ting. And

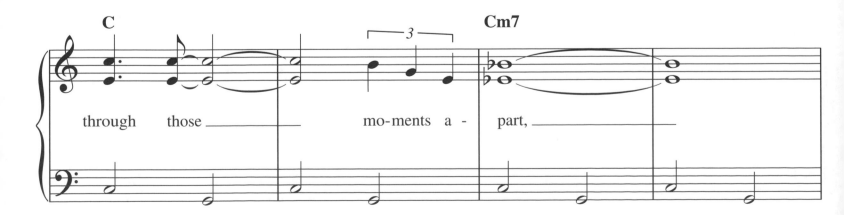

through those mo - ments a - part,

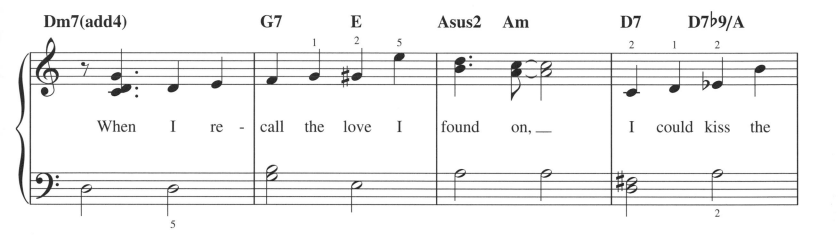

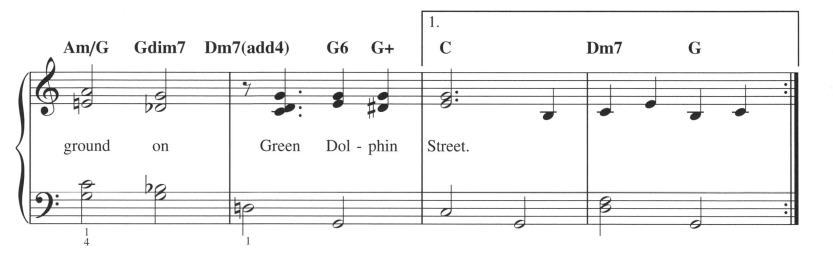

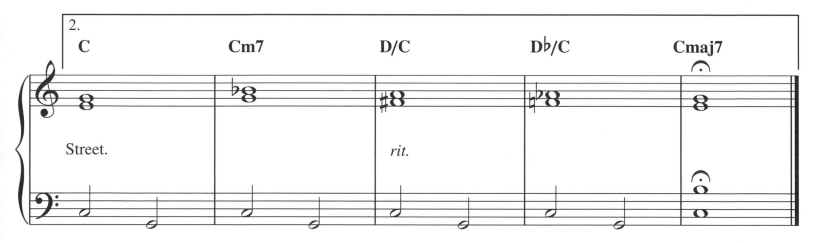

ONE O'CLOCK JUMP

By COUNT BASIE

Moderate Swing

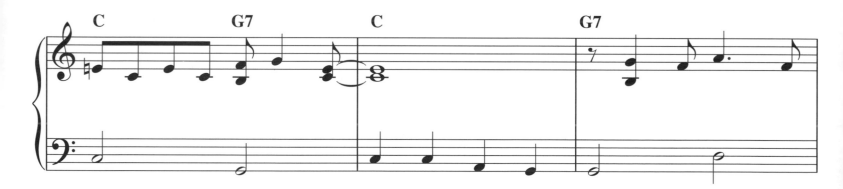

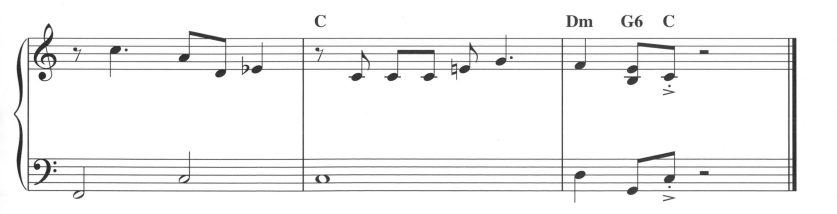

OVER THE RAINBOW
from THE WIZARD OF OZ

Music by HAROLD ARLNE
Lyric by E.Y. "YIP" HARBURG

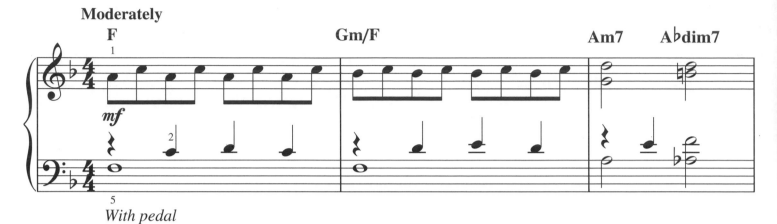

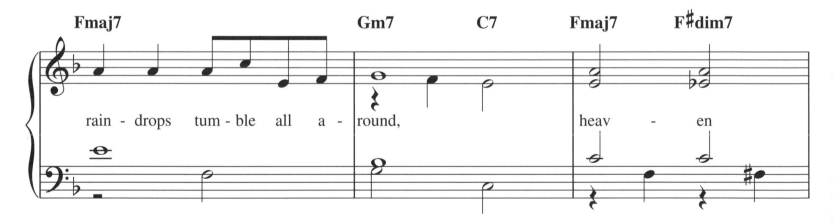

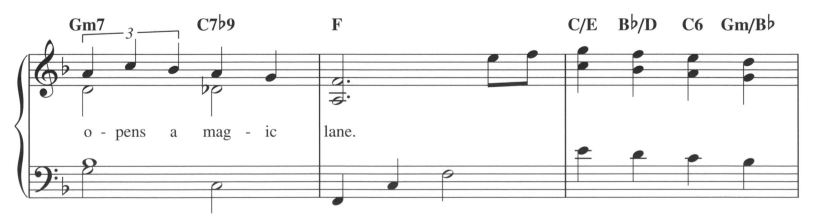

When all the clouds dark-en up the sky-way, there's a rain-bow high-way to be

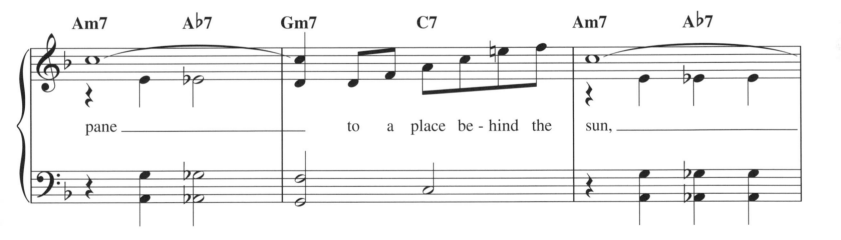

found, lead - ing from your win - dow -

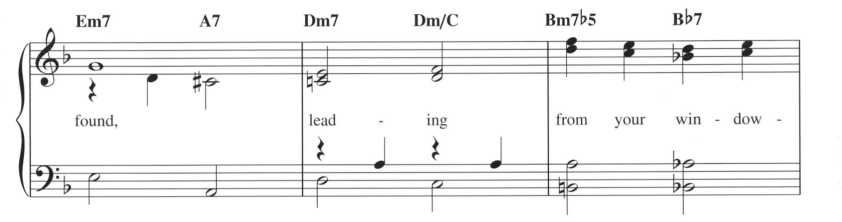

pane _____ to a place be-hind the sun, _____

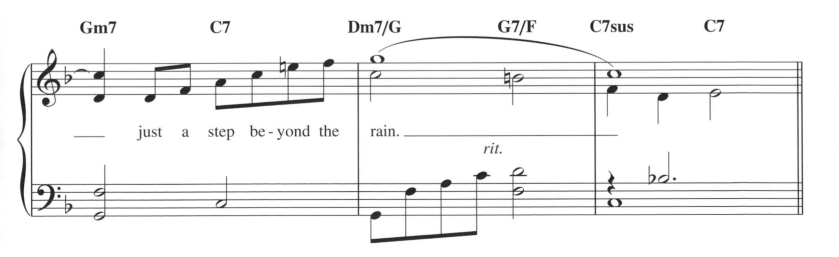

_____ just a step be-yond the rain. _____

rit.

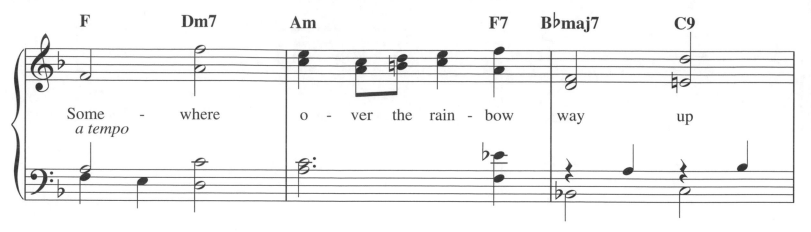

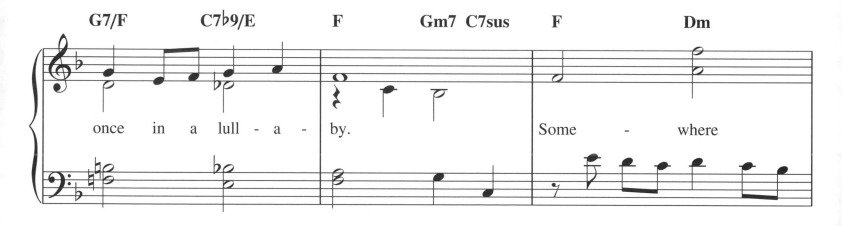

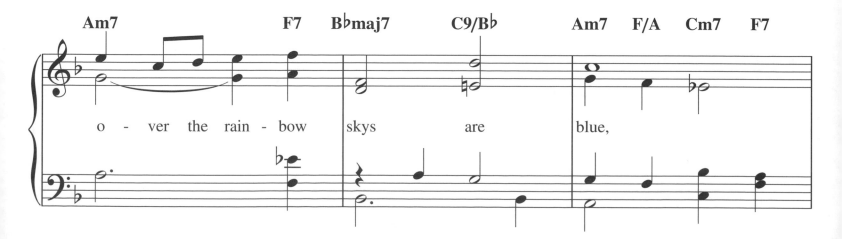

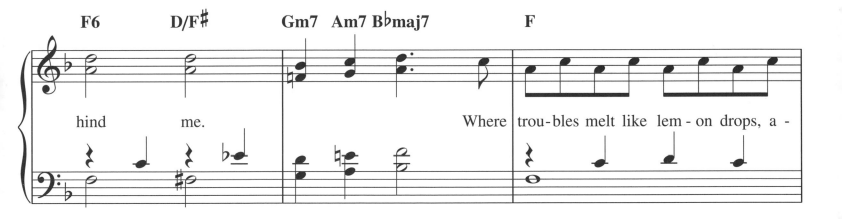

Somewhere over the rainbow bluebirds fly.

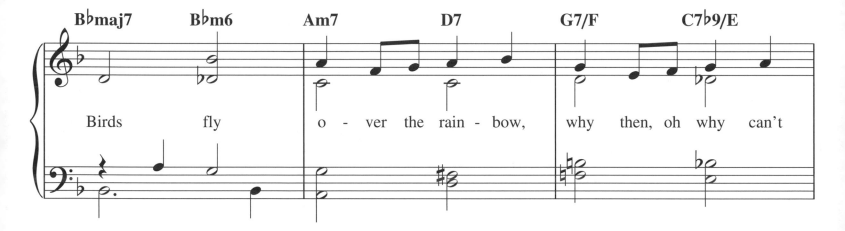

Birds fly over the rainbow, why then, oh why can't

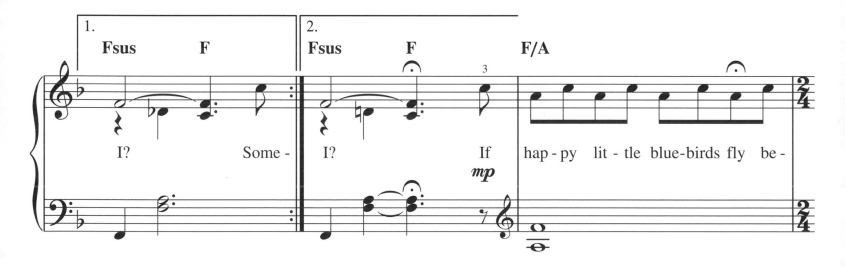

1. I? Some-
2. I? If happy little bluebirds fly be-

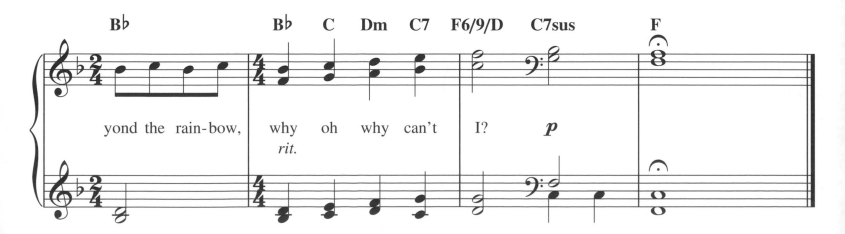

yond the rainbow, why oh why can't I?

SWEET GEORGIA BROWN

Words and Music by BEN BERNIE
MACEO PINKARD and KENNETH CASEY

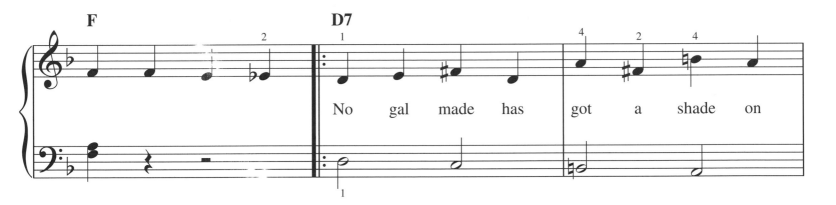

C7

They all sigh and wan - na die for sweet Geor - gia Brown, _

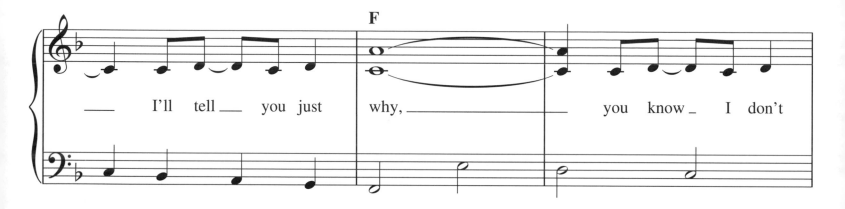

F

_ I'll tell _ you just why, _____ you know _ I don't

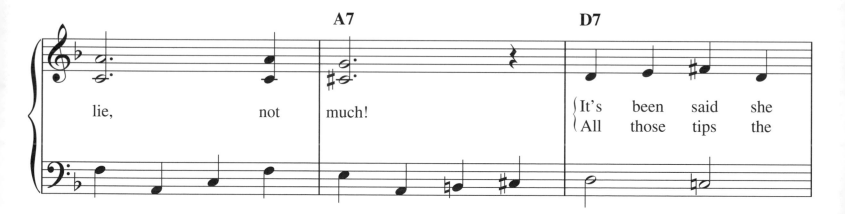

A7   **D7**

lie,   not   much!   { It's been said she
                             { All those tips the

knocks 'em dead when   she   lands in town; _
por - ter slips to   sweet   Geor - gia Brown, _

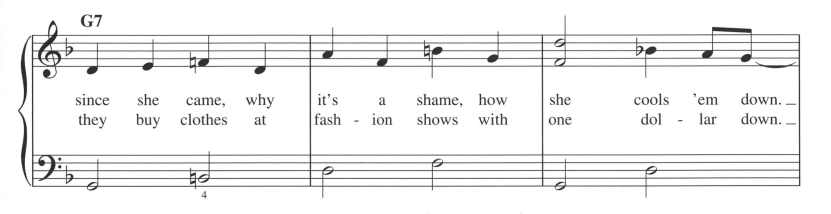

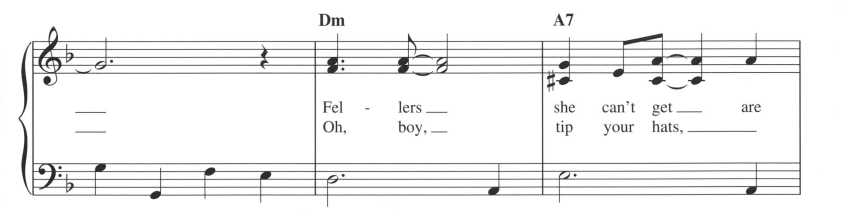

THE SHADOW OF YOUR SMILE

Love Theme from THE SANDPIPER

Music by JOHNNY MANDEL
Words by PAUL FRANCIS WEBSTER

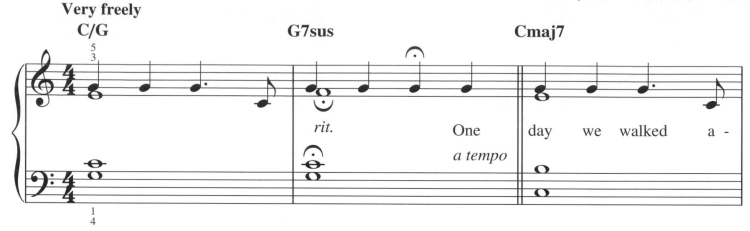

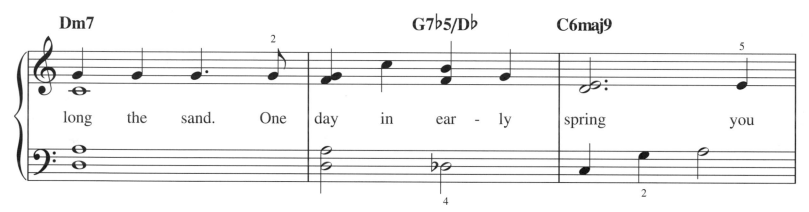

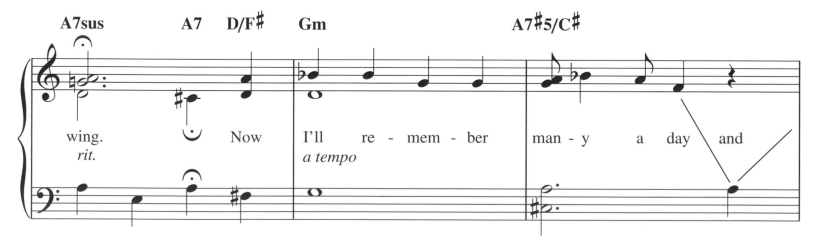

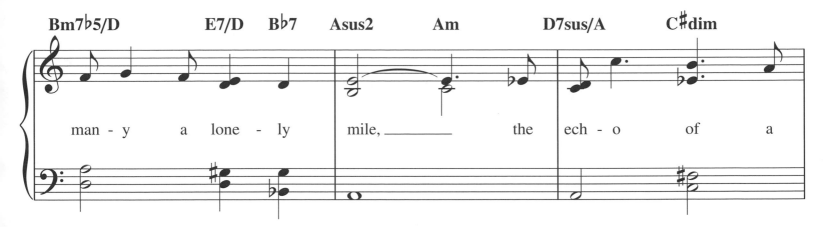

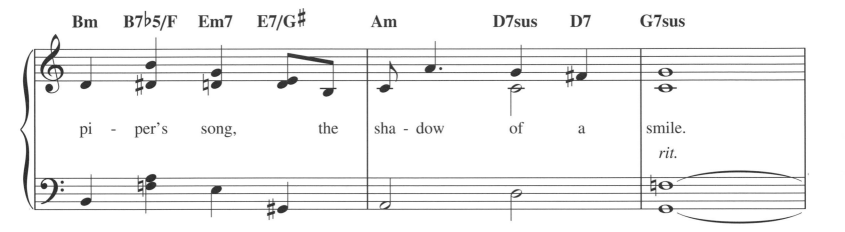

G   **C(add2)/E**   **F#dim**   **B7/D#**   **B7**

dawn.   Look in - to my eyes,   my   love,   and

Em   **Em7/D**   **C#m7♭5**   **F#7♭9**

see   all the love - ly   things   you   are   to

F#m7♭5/C   **B**   **F#m**   **B7#5**

me.   Our wist - ful lit - tle   star   was   far   too

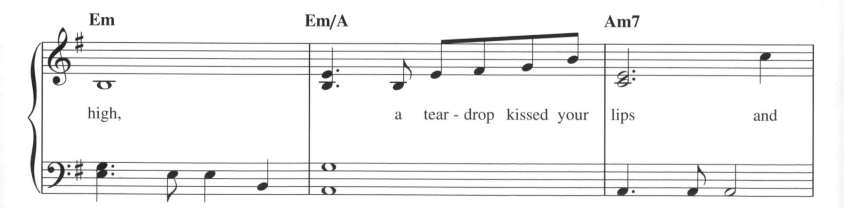

Em   **Em/A**   **Am7**

high,   a tear - drop kissed your   lips   and

so did I.   Now when I re-mem-ber spring,

all the joy that love can bring,   I will be re-

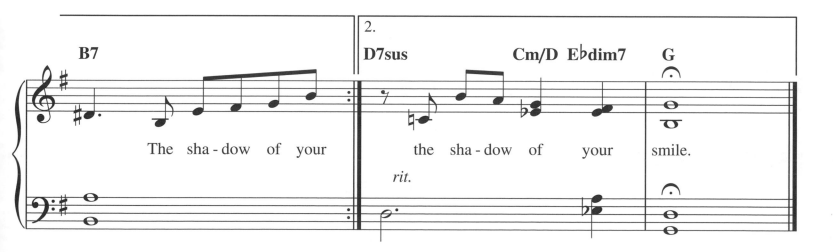

mem - ber-ing   the sha-dow of your smile.

1.

The sha-dow of your   the sha-dow of your smile.

SING, SING, SING

Words and Music by
LOUIS PRIMA

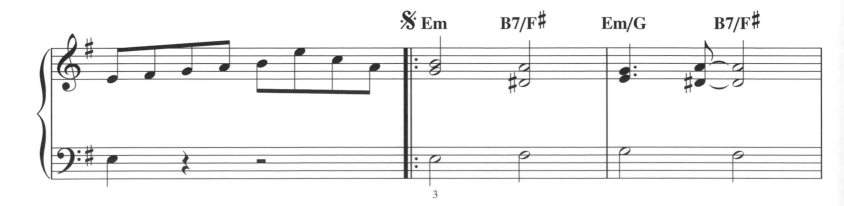

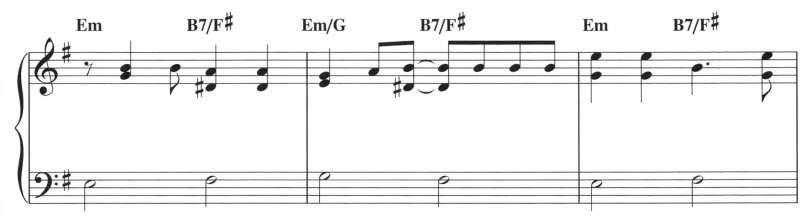

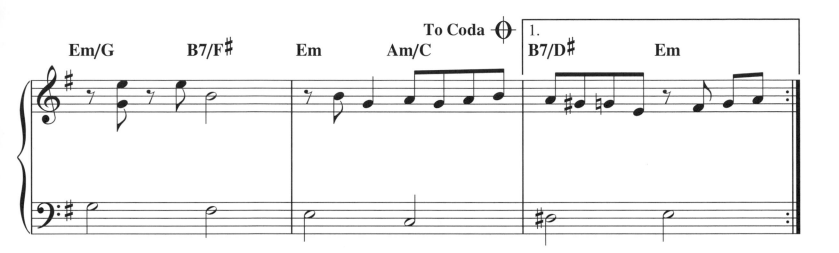

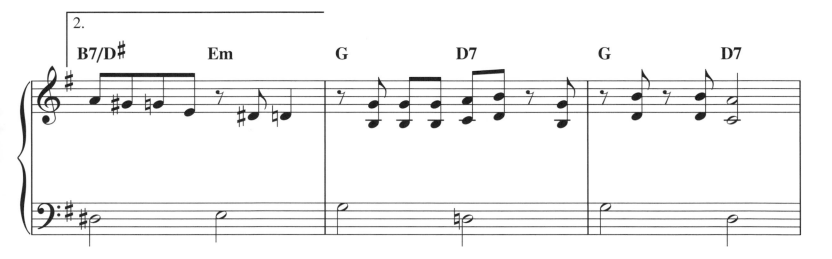

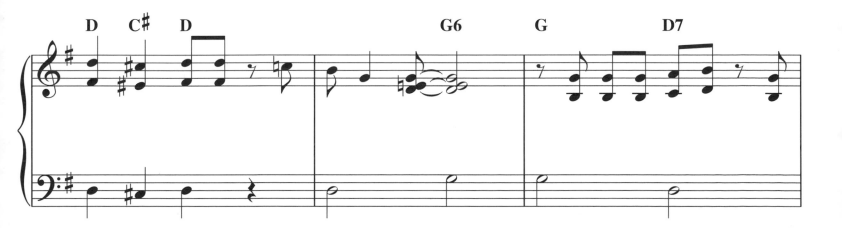

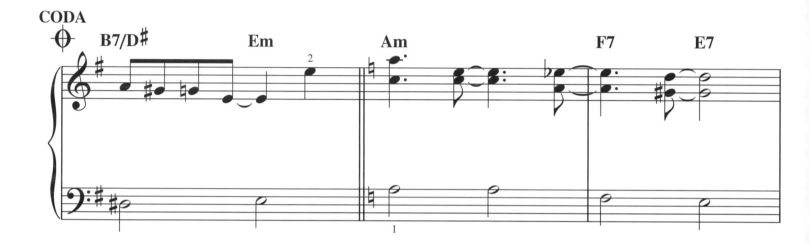

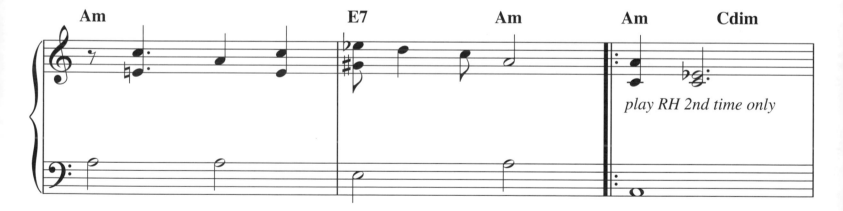

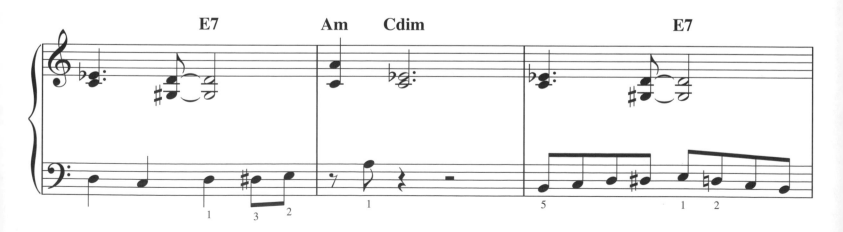

play as written both times

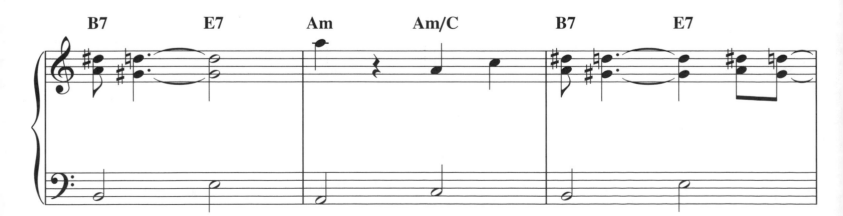

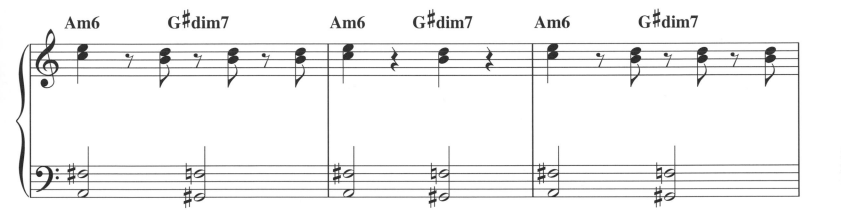

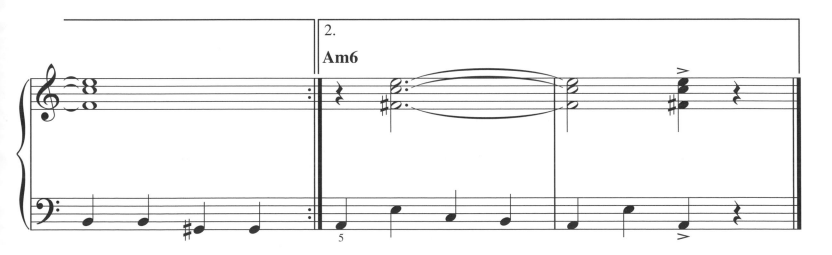

SPRING IS HERE

from I MARRIED AN ANGEL

Words by LORENZ HART
Music by RICHARD RODGERS

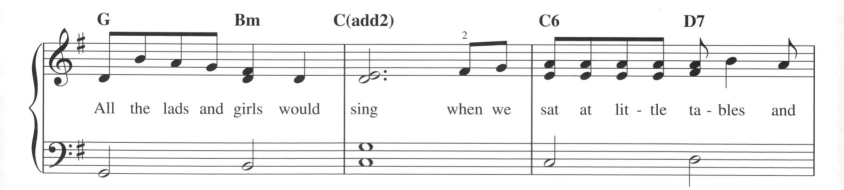

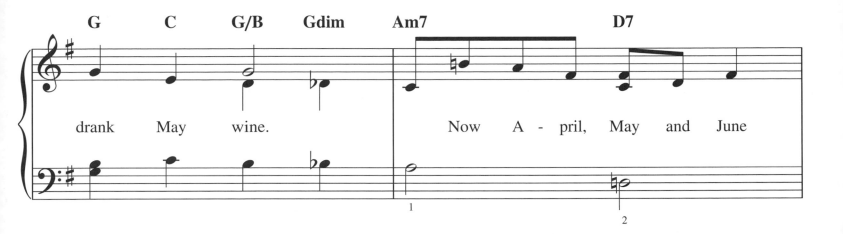

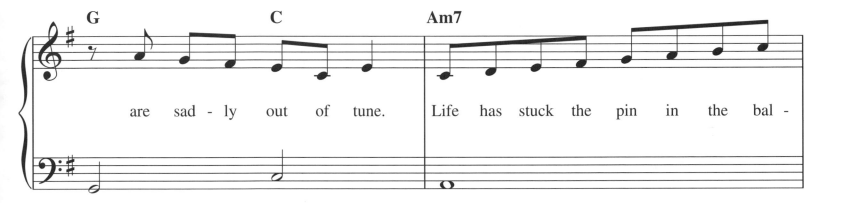

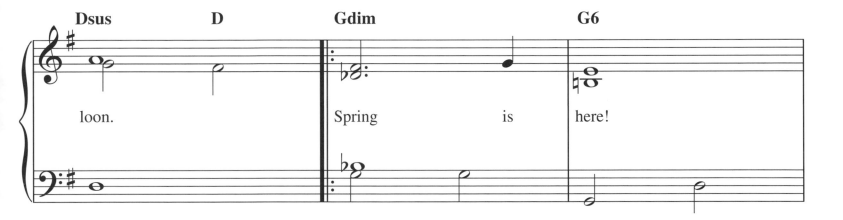

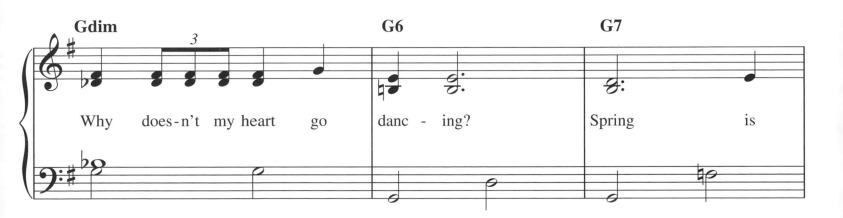

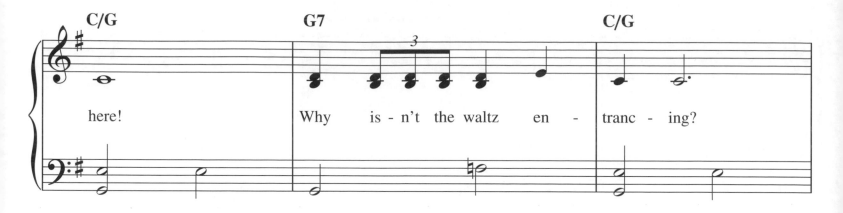

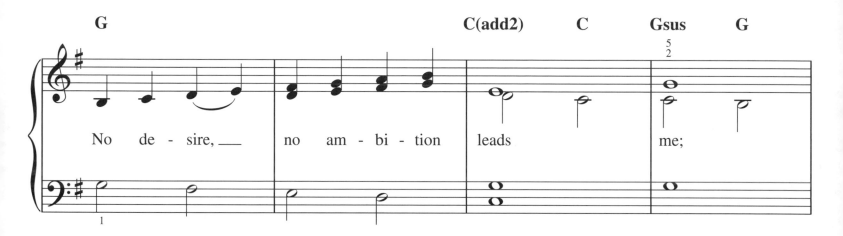

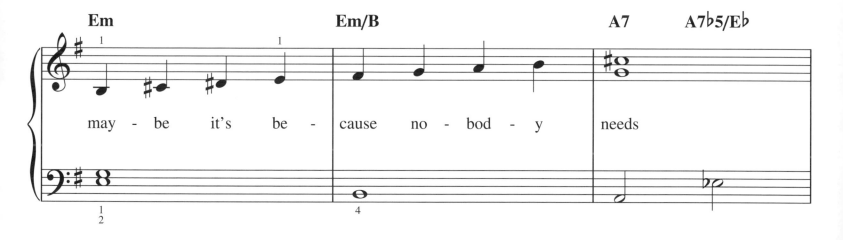

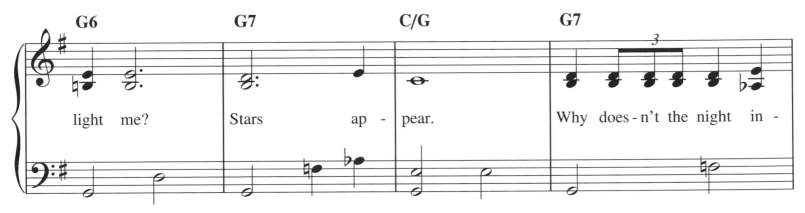

light me? Stars   ap - pear. Why does-n't the night in -

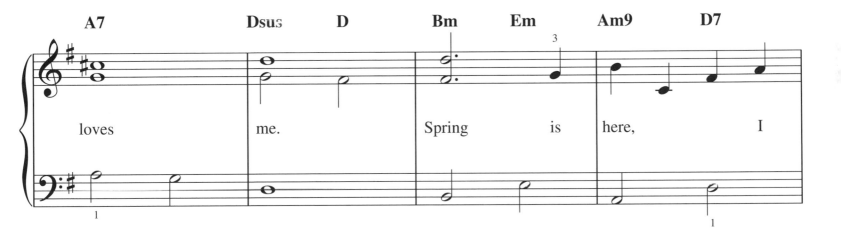

vite   me? May - be   it's   be - cause   no - bod - y

loves   me.   Spring   is   here,   I

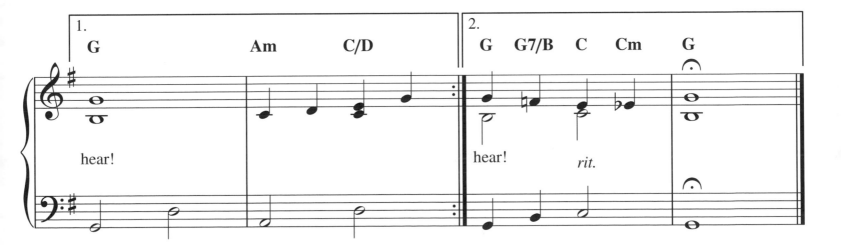

hear!   hear!   *rit.*

STAR EYES

Words by DON RAYE
Music by GENE DePAUL

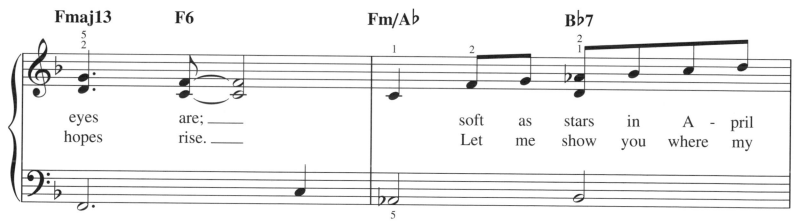

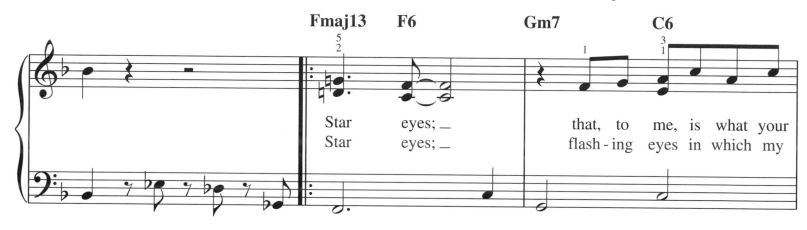

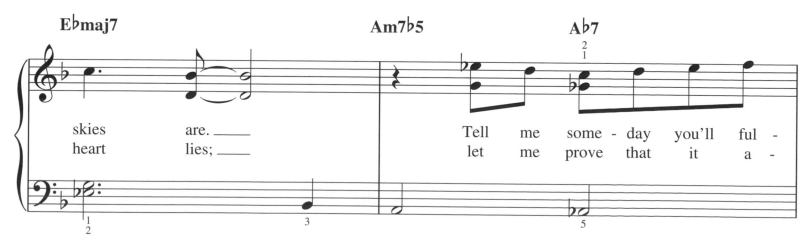

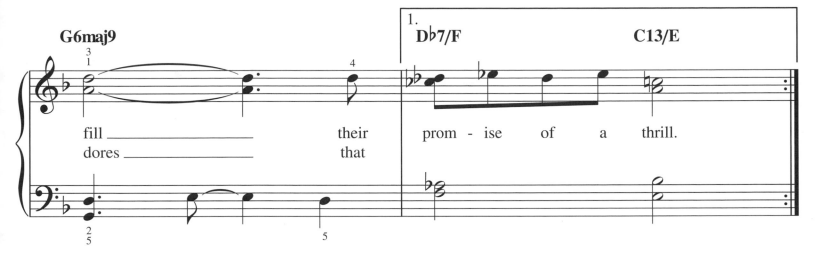

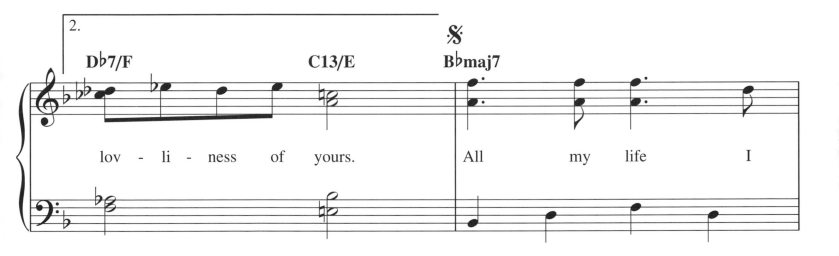

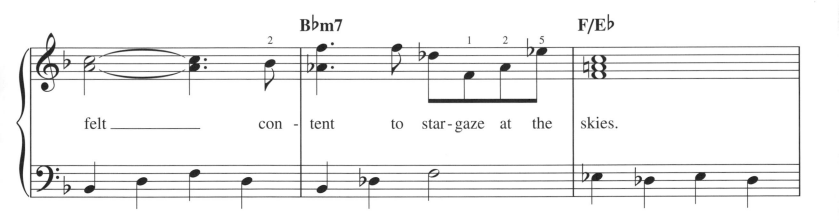

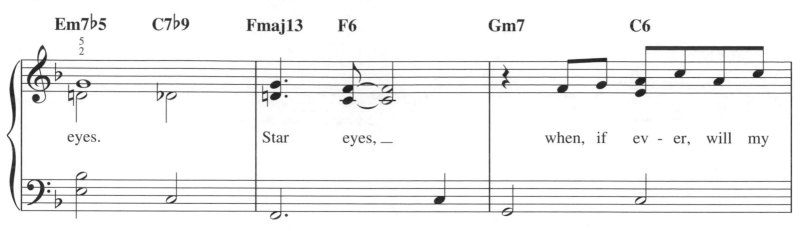

Em7♭5 C7♭9 Fmaj13 F6 Gm7 C6

eyes. Star eyes, — when, if ev - er, will my

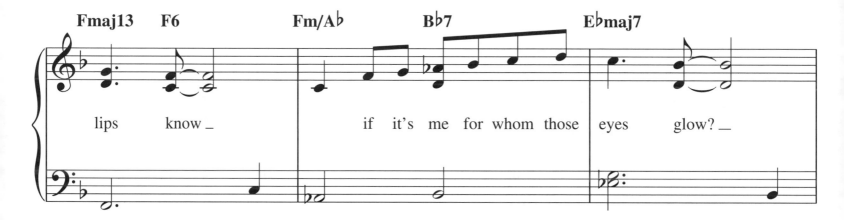

Fmaj13 F6 Fm/A♭ B♭7 E♭maj7

lips know — if it's me for whom those eyes glow? —

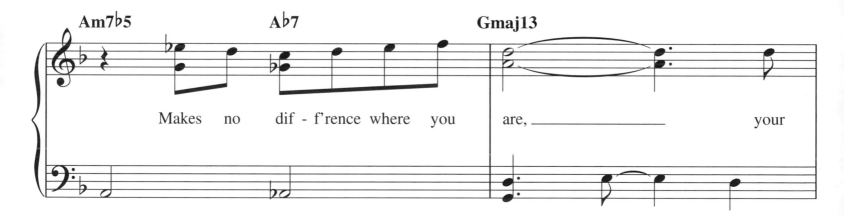

Am7♭5 A♭7 Gmaj13

Makes no dif - f'rence where you are, _____ your

To Coda ⊕

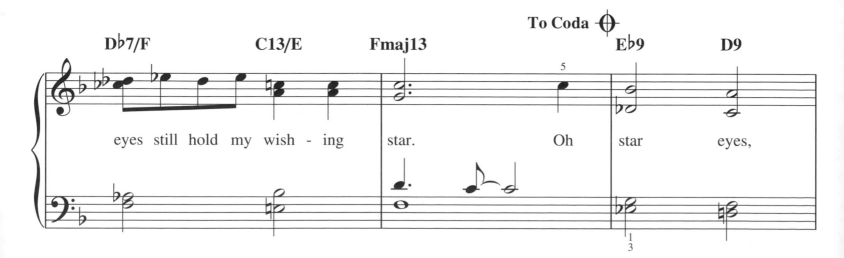

D♭7/F C13/E Fmaj13 E♭9 D9

eyes still hold my wish - ing star. Oh star eyes,

D.S. al Coda

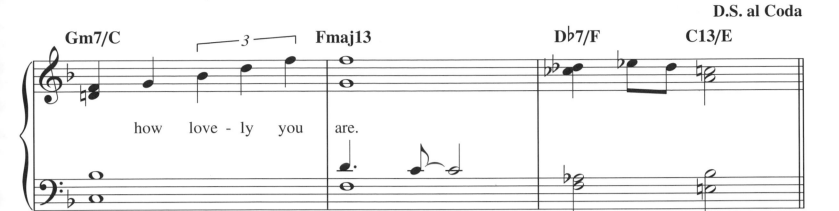

how love - ly you are.

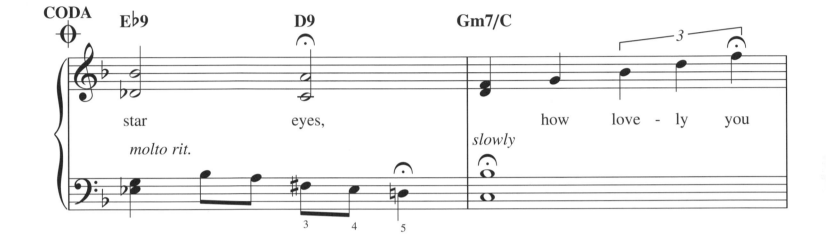

star eyes, how love - ly you

molto rit. *slowly*

are.

a tempo

TAKING A CHANCE ON LOVE

Words by JOHN LA TOUCHE and TED FETTER
Music by VERNON DUKE

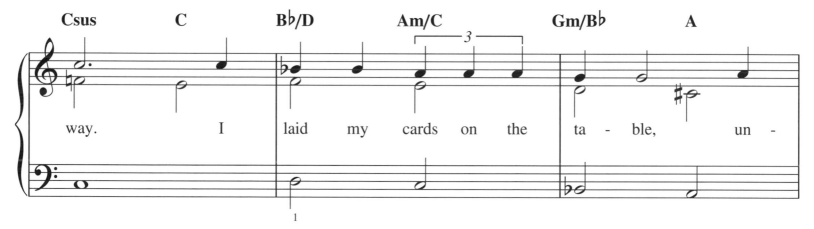

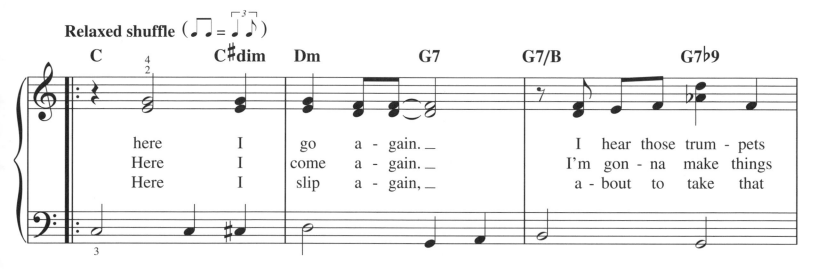

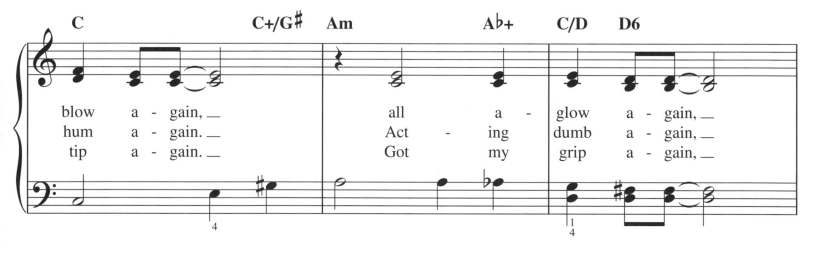

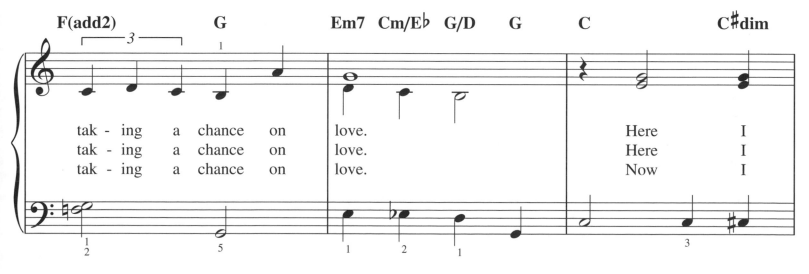

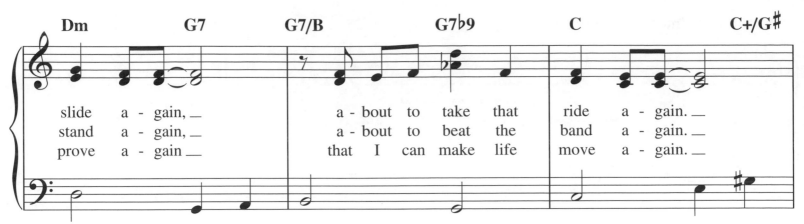

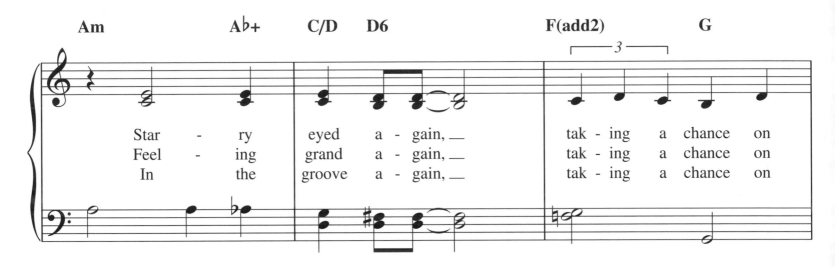

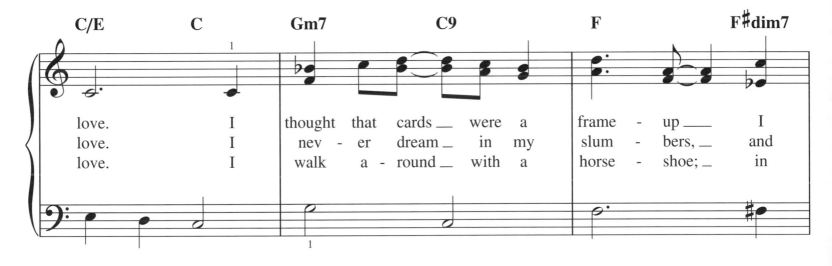

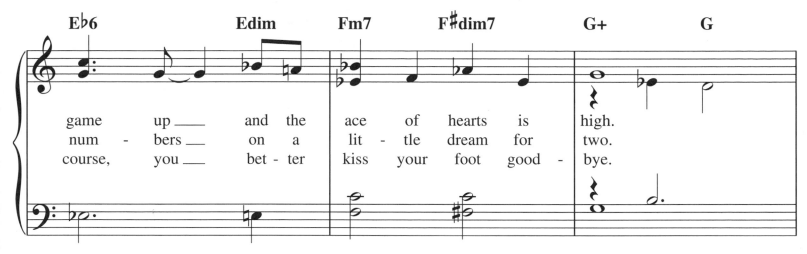

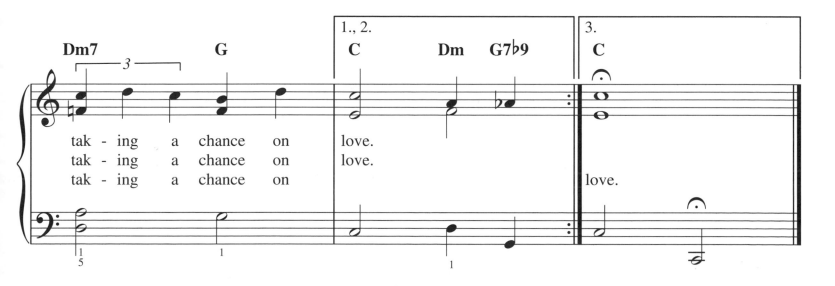

TEA FOR TWO
from NO, NO, NANETTE

Words by IRVING CAESAR
Music by VINCENT YOUMANS

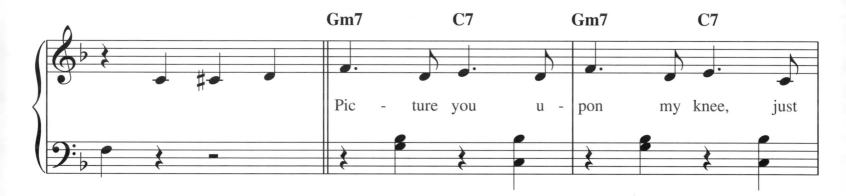

Pic - ture you u - pon my knee, just

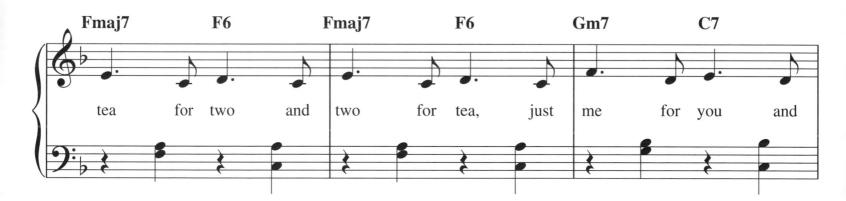

tea for two and two for tea, just me for you and

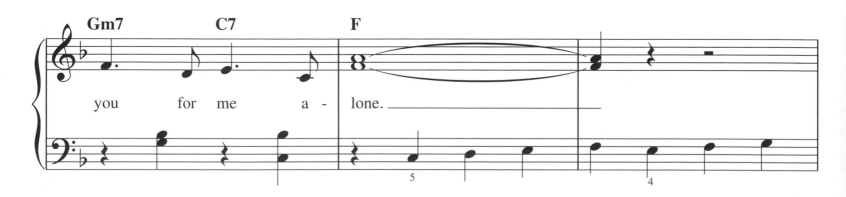

you for me a - lone.

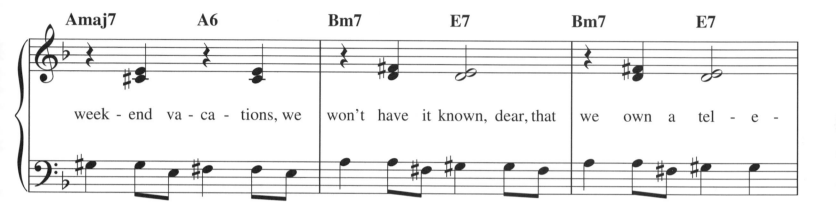

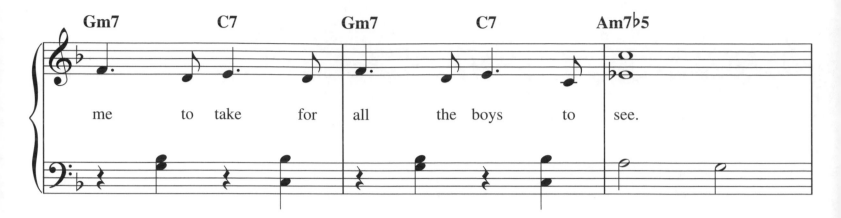

me   to take   for   all   the boys   to   see.

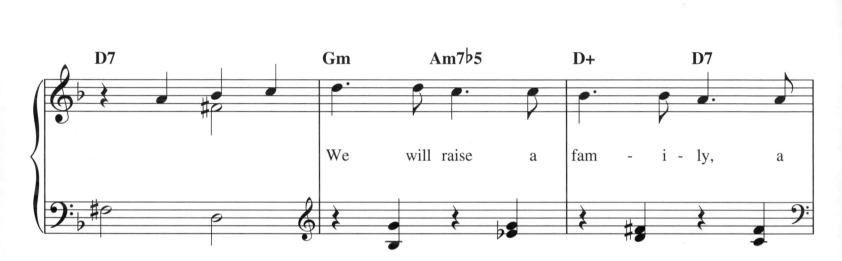

We   will raise   a   fam - i - ly,   a

boy   for you,   a   girl   for me.   Oh   can't   you see   how

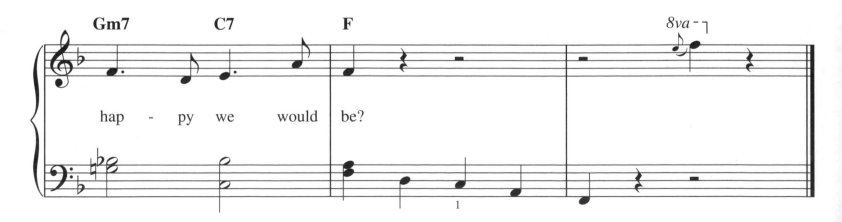

hap - py   we   would   be?

YOU AND THE NIGHT AND THE MUSIC

Words by HOWARD DIETZ
Music by ARTHUR SCHWARTZ

Dramatically, with freedom

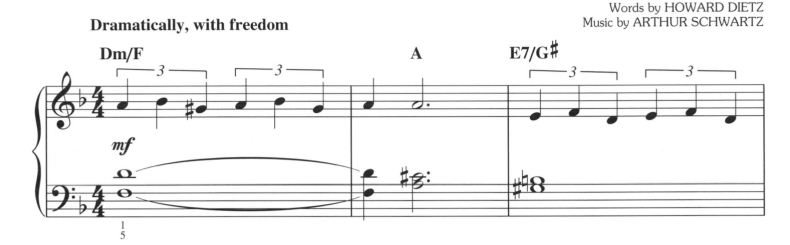

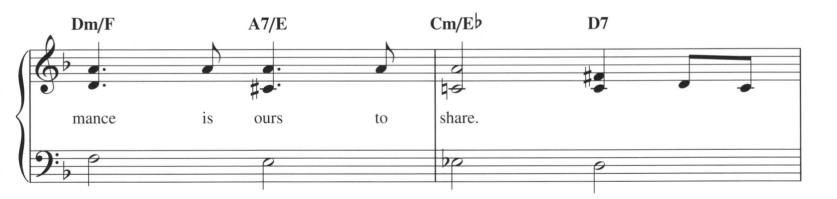

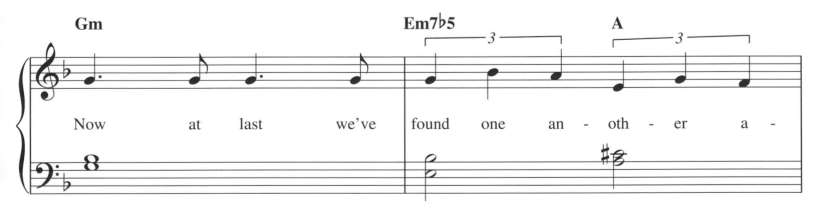

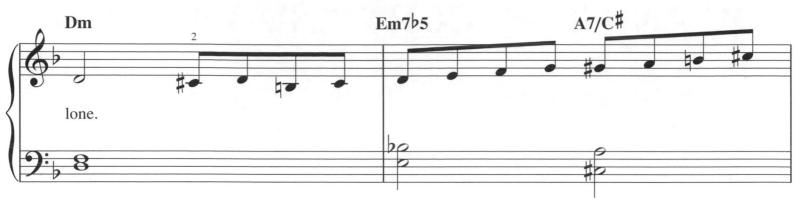

lone.

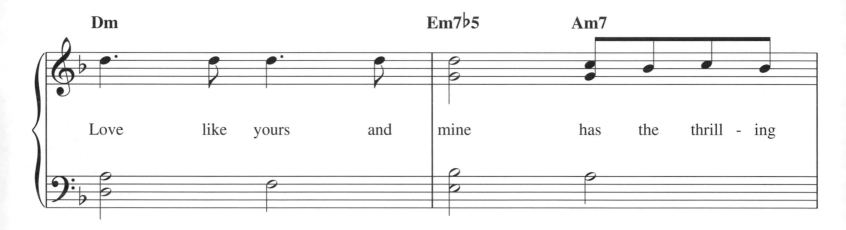

Love   like   yours   and   mine   has   the   thrill - ing

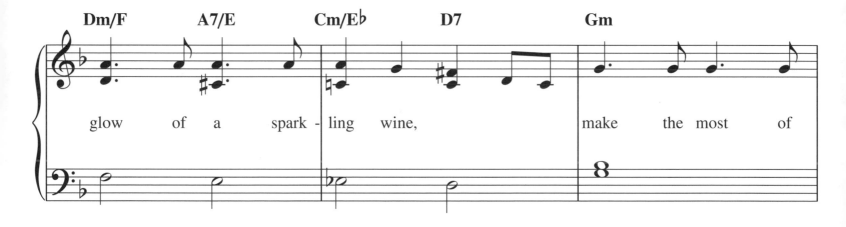

glow   of   a   spark - ling   wine,   make   the   most   of

time   ere   it   has   flown. _____

rall.

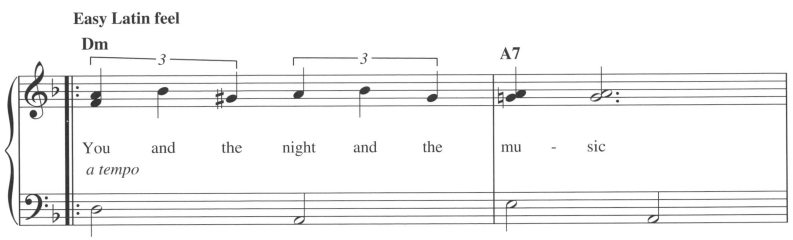

Easy Latin feel

You and the night and the mu - sic

a tempo

fill me with flam-ing de - sire, set - ting my be - ing com-

plete - ly on fire!

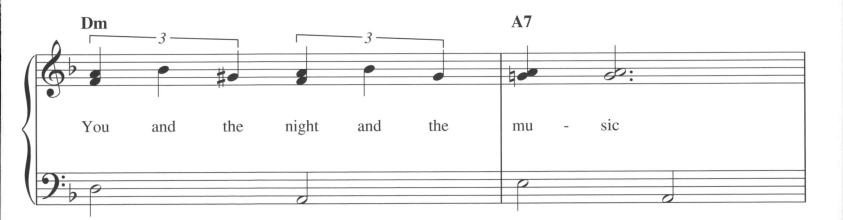

You and the night and the mu - sic

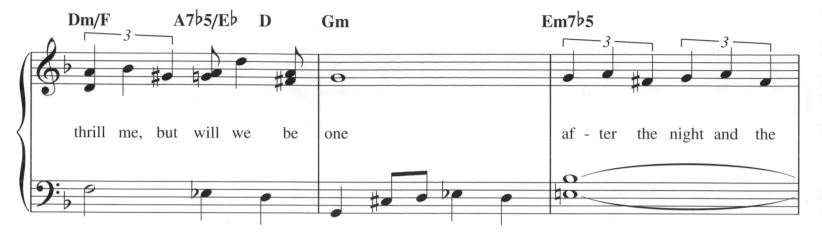

thrill me, but will we be one af - ter the night and the

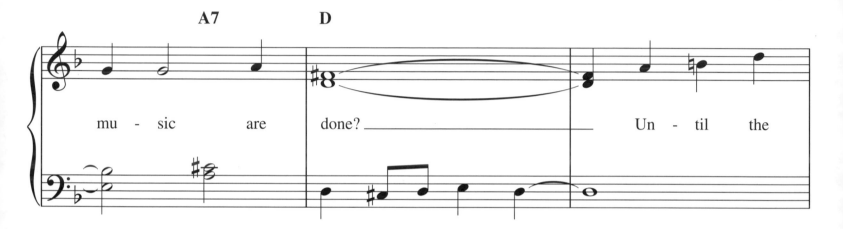

mu - sic are done?_____ Un - til the

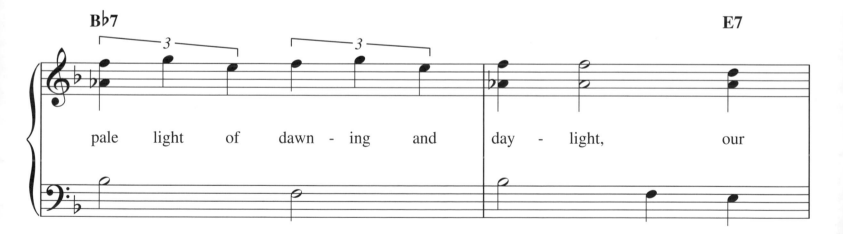

pale light of dawn - ing and day - light, our

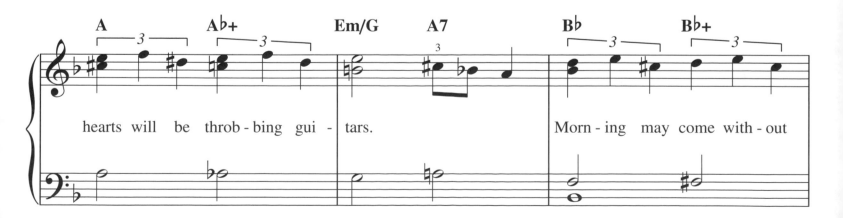

hearts will be throb - bing gui - tars. Morn - ing may come with - out

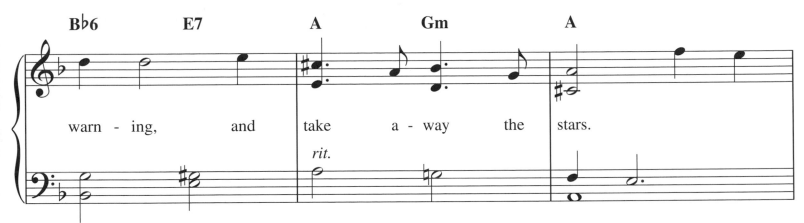

warn - ing,   and   take   a - way   the   stars.

rit.

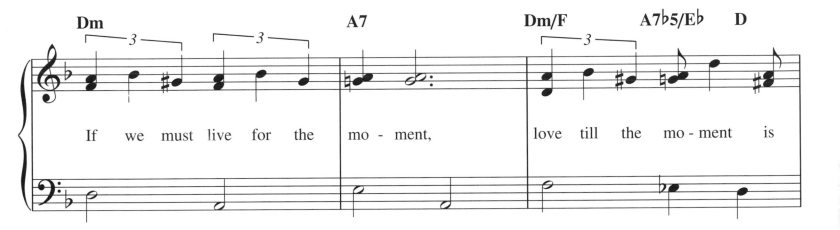

If   we   must   live   for   the   mo - ment,   love   till   the   mo - ment   is

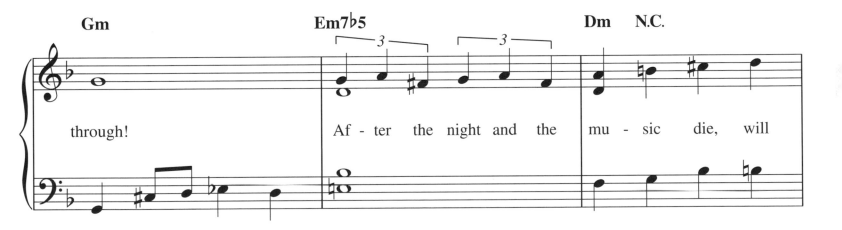

through!   Af - ter   the   night   and   the   mu - sic   die,   will

I   have   you?   you?

YOU STEPPED OUT OF A DREAM

Words by GUS KAHN
Music by NACIO HERB BROWN

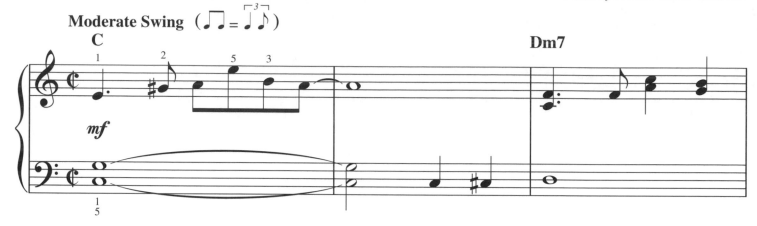

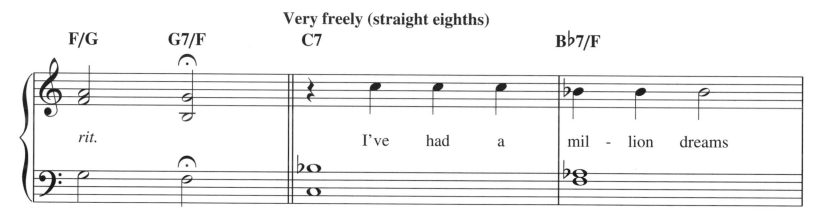

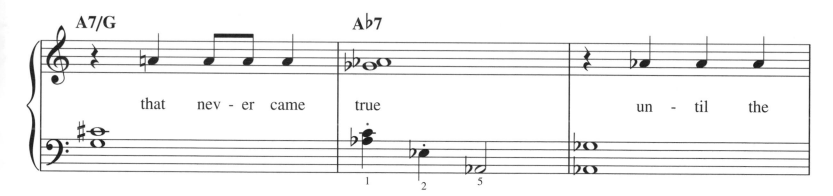

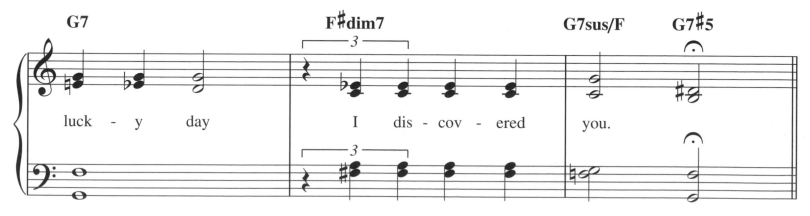

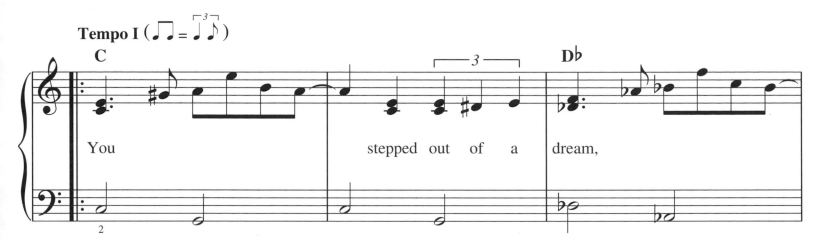

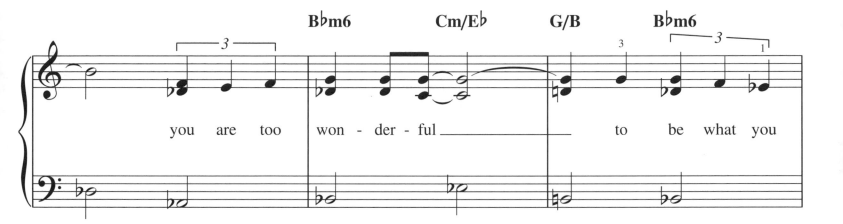

smiles like yours, _____ hon - est and trul -

y? You stepped out of a

cloud. I want to take you a - way, _____

____ a - way from the crowd and have you

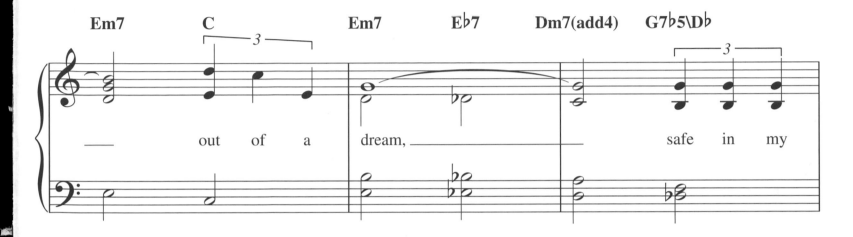

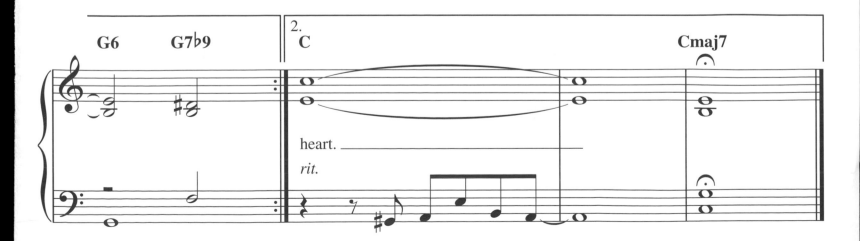

It's Easy to Play Your Favorite Songs with Hal Leonard Easy Piano Books

Beatles Best for Easy Piano
Easy arrangements of 120 Beatles hits. A truly remarkable collection including: All My Loving • And I Love Her • Come Together • Eleanor Rigby • Get Back • Help! • Hey Jude • I Want to Hold Your Hand • Let It Be • Michelle • many, many more.
00364092..............................$24.99

The Best Broadway Songs Ever
The 2nd edition of this bestseller features 65+ Broadway faves: All I Ask of You • I Wanna Be a Producer • Just in Time • My Funny Valentine • On My Own • Seasons of Love • The Sound of Music • Tomorrow • Where or When • Younger Than Springtime • more!
00300178 ....$21.99

The Best Praise & Worship Songs Ever
The name says it all: over 70 of the best P&W songs today. Titles include: Awesome God • Blessed Be Your Name • Come, Now Is the Time to Worship • Days of Elijah • Here I Am to Worship • Open the Eyes of My Heart • Shout to the Lord • We Fall Down • and more.
00311312..............................$19.99

The Best Songs Ever
Over 70 all-time favorite songs, including: All I Ask of You • Body and Soul • Call Me Irresponsible • Edelweiss • Fly Me to the Moon • The Girl from Ipanema • Here's That Rainy Day • Imagine • Let It Be • Moonlight in Vermont • People • Somewhere Out There • Tears in Heaven • Unforgettable • The Way We Were • and more.
00359223..............................$19.95

Get complete song lists and more at **www.halleonard.com**
Prices, contents, and availability subject to change without notice

Disney characters and artwork © Disney Enterprises, Inc.

Ten Top Hits for Easy Piano
Ten tunes from the top of the charts in 2006: Because of You • Black Horse and the Cherry Tree • Breaking Free • Jesus Take the Wheel • Listen to Your Heart • Over My Head (Cable Car) • The Riddle • Unwritten • Upside Down • You're Beautiful.
00310530..............................$10.95

Jumbo Easy Piano Songbook
200 classical favorites, folk songs and jazz standards. Includes: Amazing Grace • Beale Street Blues • Bridal Chorus • Buffalo Gals • Canon in D • Cielito Lindo • Danny Boy • The Entertainer • Für Elise • Greensleeves • Jamaica Farewell • Marianne • Molly Malone • Ode to Joy • Peg O' My Heart • Rockin' Robin • Yankee Doodle • dozens more!
00311014..............................$19.99

Best Children's Songs Ever
A great collection of over 100 songs, including: Alphabet Song • The Bare Necessities • Beauty and the Beast • Eensy Weensy Spider • The Farmer in the Dell • Hakuna Matata • My Favorite Things • Puff the Magic Dragon • The Rainbow Connection • Take Me Out to the Ball Game • Twinkle, Twinkle Little Star • Winnie the Pooh • and more.
00310360..............................$19.95

150 of the Most Beautiful Songs Ever
Easy arrangements of 150 of the most popular songs of our time. Includes: Bewitched • Fly Me to the Moon • How Deep Is Your Love • My Funny Valentine • Some Enchanted Evening • Tears in Heaven • Till There Was You • Yesterday • You Are So Beautiful • and more. 550 pages of great music!
00311316..............................$24.95

50 Easy Classical Themes
Easy arrangements of 50 classical tunes representing more than 30 composers, including: Bach, Beethoven, Chopin, Debussy, Dvorak, Handel, Haydn, Liszt, Mozart, Mussorgsky, Puccini, Rossini, Schubert, Strauss, Tchaikovsky, Vivaldi, and more.
00311215..............................$12.95

Today's Country Hits
A collection of 13 contemporary country favorites, including: Bless the Broken Road • Jesus Take the Wheel • Summertime • Tonight I Wanna Cry • When I Get Where I'm Goin' • When the Stars Go Blue • and more.
00290188..............................$12.95

VH1's 100 Greatest Songs of Rock and Roll
The results from the VH1 show that featured the 100 greatest rock and roll songs of all time are here in this awesome collection! Songs include: Born to Run • Good Vibrations • Hey Jude • Hotel California • Imagine • Light My Fire • Like a Rolling Stone • Respect • and more.
00311110..............................$27.95

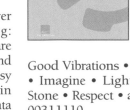

Disney's My First Song Book
16 favorite songs to sing and play. Every page is beautifully illustrated with full-color art from Disney features. Songs include: Beauty and the Beast • Bibbidi-Bobbidi-Boo • Circle of Life • Cruella De Vil • A Dream Is a Wish Your Heart Makes • Hakuna Matata • Under the Sea • Winnie the Pooh • You've Got a Friend in Me • and more.
00310322..............................$16.99

HAL•LEONARD® CORPORATION
7777 W. BLUEMOUND RD. P.O. BOX 13819 MILWAUKEE, WI 53213

0512